95

D1107899

WITHDRAWN

745.928 SHE 1988

CARSON CITY LIBRARY
900 North Roop Street
Carson City, NV 89701
775-887-2244

Pressed Flowers

Pressed
Flowers

CREATING AND STYLING

Joanna Sheen

DAVID R. GODINE
—— BOSTON ——

First U.S. edition published in 1988 by
David R. Godine, Publisher, Inc.
Horticultural Hall
300 Massachusetts Avenue
Boston, Massachusetts 02115

Originally published in
the U.K. by
Merehurst Press, London

© Copyright 1988 Merehurst Limited

ISBN 0 87923 766 X

Library of Congress Catalog Card Number 88 45366

All rights reserved. No part of this
publication may be reproduced, stored in a
retrieval system, or transmitted in any
form or by any means, electronic,
mechanical, photocopying, recording or
otherwise, without the prior written
permission of the copyright owner.

Edited by Jane Struthers
Designed by Peartree Design Associates
Arrangements photographed by Steve Lee,
assisted by Cliff Morgan
Styling by Joanna Sheen, assisted by
Barbara Stewart and Lesley Harrod
Typeset by Rowland Phototypesetting Limited
Bury St Edmunds, Suffolk
Colour separation by Fotographics Limited
London-Hong Kong
Printed by New Interlitho S.p.A., Milan

To Adrian, without whom there wouldn't have
been a book

My thanks to Margaret Thorpe for making the
two lovely wedding bouquets and to Jane
Struthers, Jane Donovan, Lesley Harrod,
Steve Lee and Cliff Morgan – not forgetting
all the staff of Joanna Sheen Limited – for
all their help in the production of this
book.

Printed in Italy

CONTENTS

FOREWORD

This is a book that cannot fail to please. It brings to the reach of everyone interested in flowers and decorative work a very special product – a revival of the art carried out many years ago and now back in the limelight, thanks to the wonderful work carried out by such people as Joanna Sheen and her staff.

Those of you who have visited recent Chelsea Flower Shows must remember the crowds of people gathered around Joanna's stand all day long, trying to see her excellent displays – a sure sign of the interest taken today in this form of decoration.

I felt very honoured when I was asked to write a few lines as the foreword to this new book and it is with pleasure that I do so. Many writers have touched upon this subject but to my knowledge there has never before been a book that covered the topic in so much detail.

I am always so happy to see any of my old students doing well in their chosen career and finding satisfaction from the hard work that they put in at the Constance Spry Flower School in the early days of their basic training. It is even more pleasing to find one who breaks away from the true commercial floristry and makes a name for herself in a specialist field.

This book, with its pages full of every detail, will prove to be a most useful and valuable addition to the library of every flower arranger.

Harold Piercy
N.D.H., Dip.Ed. (B'ham)

CHAPTER ONE

CHOOSING YOUR PRESSING MATERIAL

There is a wealth of different flowers and foliage that can be pressed and used to make stunning pictures, but it is important to know which plants press well and which do not. As well as detailing concrete guidelines for the beginner, this chapter also allows plenty of scope for experimentation.

THE BEAUTY OF FLOWERS

The world would be a very dismal place if we had to live without flowers and attractive foliage. Whatever the weather, one's mood or problems, everyone smiles when they are given flowers. Walking around a garden that's in full bloom is one of the most exciting, yet relaxing, of pastimes, with the riot of colour and scents a continual delight.

Although plants and flowers can be quite breathtaking when viewed *en masse*, there is a quiet beauty in looking carefully at a single flower. One of the unexpected joys of pressing flowers is that one gets to know particular species and leaves far more intimately than would have been possible when passing a whole bed of flowers in a garden. Sometimes the rarely glimpsed underside of a leaf is far more interesting than its top, and dismantling a flower in order to press its petals individually can reveal all sorts of treasures: the centres of flowers, the sepals and stamens all have a particular beauty of their own.

The saddest part of having fresh flowers around the house or growing in the garden is that they will gradually wilt and die. However, that is not the case with pressed flowers, although you may have to pick them in their prime and keep them hidden for at least a couple of months. Once they are ready they can be incorporated into a piece of pressed flower work and enjoyed by everyone for a very long time. That seems much better value for a beautiful flower than if it only lasts a few days. Never think what a pity it is to pick flowers in perfect condition in order to press them – rather, think of it as immortalising your best specimens!

Preserving flowers is far from being a modern art – the real enthusiasm for flower pressing took place in Victorian times. Then, there were several reasons for pressing flowers, one of which was botanical: young ladies would wander along lanes and through fields during the year and keep a permanent and decorative record of the plants that they found. Flowers were also pressed for technical purposes, and specimen plants were preserved as a botanical record during specialist plant-collecting trips. With the Victorian passion for memorabilia, another reason for pressing flowers was purely sentimental. A rose could be picked from a garden by an admirer and then pressed between the pages of the family bible, or flowers could be kept as a memorial to someone special. For example, Queen Victoria pressed a great many flowers, amongst which were those from Prince Albert's funeral.

In common with many other pastimes popular during Victorian times, the art of pressing flowers requires plenty of patience, particularly if you want a perfect result. It seems a waste of effort to approach a craft like this in a half-hearted manner, and if the completed work is to be of a high standard then you must exercise extreme patience at every stage, even if you are eager to see the finished result. For example, if there is a leaf out of place or a smear under the glass, then it must be altered or cleaned: in the same way that a slipped stitch will always show in a piece of knitting, so an uncorrected error will always be clearly seen in the picture and spoil your long-term enjoyment.

Flower pressing has gained new popularity in the last few years, as has the craft of drying flowers. With the arrival of central heating in most homes, fresh flowers do not last as long as they once did, so many people are looking for other ways of enjoying flowers. If one gathers a good crop of blooms during the summer and keeps them in the presses until the dark evenings start to draw in and they are ready to be used, then the joy of summer flowers can remain all through the winter. Pressed flowers are also very useful when it comes

The Victorians made a true art from pressed flowers, as it suited their love of memorabilia. Here, pansies, a foxglove and some white clover have been pressed between the pages of an old book.

to special occasions. After all, everyone likes flowers, so lovely flowers and a gift that you have made yourself is an unbeatable combination. There is something very special about a present that has taken someone a lot of time, not only to choose but also to plan and actually make themselves, and these are the kinds of gift that will be treasured for a lifetime.

With a minimal amount of expense, flowers can be perfectly pressed, and creations that will please and amaze not only your friends and relatives but also yourself can be made with a little thought, some planning and careful preparation and a great deal of patience.

This arrangement shows a few of the many flowers that can be pressed successfully. It includes spray carnations, mimosa, several varieties of rose, hyacinths, lilies, daffodils and freesias.

FLOWERS SUITABLE FOR PRESSING

FLOWER	COLOUR	METHOD
Alchemilla	Yellow	Presses
Alyssum	Purple/white	Presses
Anemones	All types	Books
Anthemis	Yellow/white	Very heavy weights
Astrantia	Cream	Presses
Blossoms	Most varieties	Books
Candytuft	All colours	Presses
Carnations	Dark-edged	Petals in books
Clematis	Small dark varieties	Books
Cosmos	All colours	Books
Daisies	Small	Presses
Delphiniums	Blue	Presses
Forget-me-nots	Blue	Presses
Freesias	All colours	Books
Fritillaria	Purple	Books
Fuchsia	Small outdoor	Presses
Geum	Red	Books
Heather	All colours	Presses
Hellebores	All varieties	Books
Heuchera	Red	Presses
Honeysuckle	All varieties	Books
Hyacinth	Various	Books
Hydrangeas	Red/green	Books

FLOWER	COLOUR	METHOD
Larkspur	Pink/blue/white	Presses
Lily of the valley	White	Presses
Montbretia	Orange	Books
Narcissus	Yellow	Books
Pansy (viola)	All colours	Books
Phlox	Red/pink	Books
Potentilla	Yellow/red	Presses
Primula	Red/orange	Books
Saxifrage	Red/white	Presses
Snowdrop	White	Presses
Verbena	Red/pink	Presses
Roses		
Floribunda	All colours	Petals in books
Hybrid tea	All colours	Petals in books
Miniature	Yellow/red	Presses
Patio	Pink/red	Presses
Single/species	Yellow/red/white	Books

Foliage can play a very important role in pressed flower pictures. Amongst the suitable foliage and herbs shown here are mimosa, gypsophila, eucalyptus, cyclamen, rose and ivy leaves, and several ferns.

LEAVES, FOLIAGE AND HERBS SUITABLE FOR PRESSING

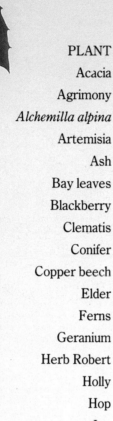

PLANT	PRESSING METHOD	COMMENTS
Acacia	Heavy press	And flowers
Agrimony	Presses	And flowers
Alchemilla alpina	Books	
Artemisia	Books	Flowers and leaves
Ash	Presses	New shoots
Bay leaves	Books	Small
Blackberry	Presses	Useful all year
Clematis	Books	And tendrils
Conifer	Presses	Small pieces – blue
Copper beech	Presses	
Elder	Presses	With flowers
Ferns	Presses	Brown/green
Geranium	Presses	Small multi-coloured
Herb Robert	Books	When red
Holly	Heavy press	New leaves
Hop	Presses	Male flowers
Ivy	Heavy press	
Japanese maple	Books	
Maple	Presses	
Mugwort	Books	Flowers and leaves
Nettle	Presses	With flowers (and gloves)
Oak	Presses	Smallest leaves

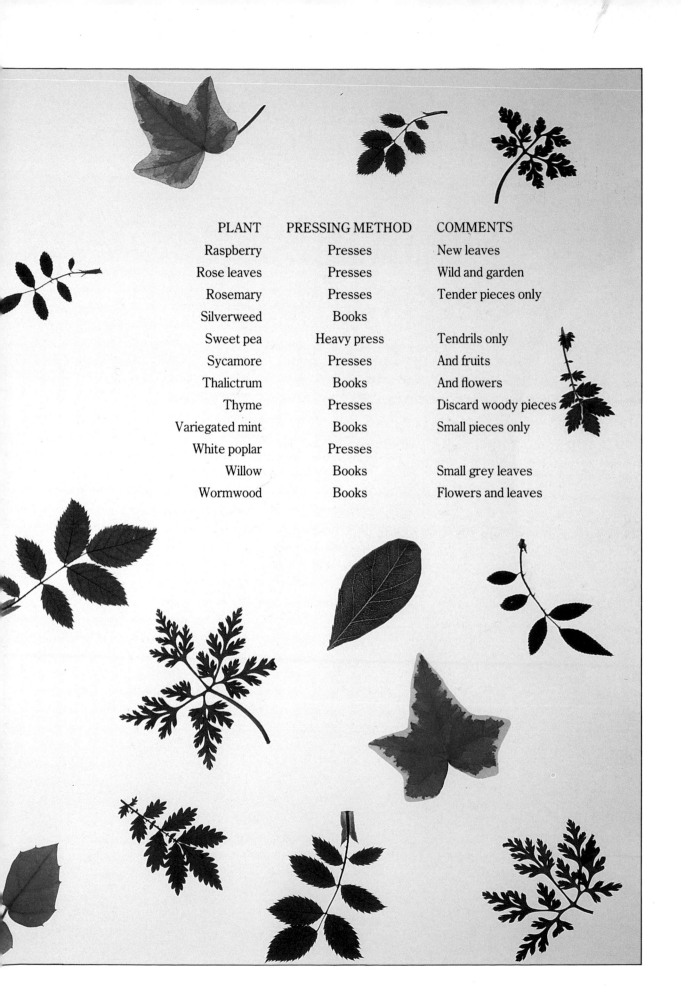

PLANT	PRESSING METHOD	COMMENTS
Raspberry	Presses	New leaves
Rose leaves	Presses	Wild and garden
Rosemary	Presses	Tender pieces only
Silverweed	Books	
Sweet pea	Heavy press	Tendrils only
Sycamore	Presses	And fruits
Thalictrum	Books	And flowers
Thyme	Presses	Discard woody pieces
Variegated mint	Books	Small pieces only
White poplar	Presses	
Willow	Books	Small grey leaves
Wormwood	Books	Flowers and leaves

CHAPTER TWO

FLOWERS TO GROW IN THE GARDEN

Gardening is a very satisfying hobby for many people. A love of gardening easily combines with the craft of flower pressing, as one leads naturally into the other. This chapter includes several suggestions for growing suitable plants for pressing in your garden, plus plenty of ideas if you would like to grow plants but don't have the luxury of a lot of space. Basically, all you need to grow flowers for pressing is a window sill or even a grow-bag!

PLANTING BY COLOUR AND SEASON

Once you have been bitten by the flower pressing bug, you will have no difficulty at all in choosing the prime specimens from your garden for hiding away in the presses. The main problem is usually an overwhelming desire to press the prize specimens from all your friends' and neighbours' gardens as well!

If you don't want to strip your garden of all colour during the summer, it is a good idea to reserve a particular area or flower bed for the plants you are intending to press. (Since you are bound to have failures as well as successes, you must always press more flowers than you think you will need.) That way, you won't feel too badly about picking flowers that have only just opened, and the rest of your garden will be left in all its glory. Nevertheless, if you pick the required specimens carefully, you'll be able to remove several leaves or flowers from, for instance, a bush in full bloom without spoiling its appearance or harming it. In many cases, and especially with annuals and some other flowering plants, picking the flowers will actually encourage more to grow, so you may find that picking for pressing can be an advantage at times.

Although pressing is easiest whenever there is least rain, because the drier the plant the better it will press, it is still perfectly possible to press specimens all the year round. The garden will be much more interesting if there is always something to watch out for, whatever the season.

One flower that appears when little else is in bloom is the hellebore, also known as the Christmas rose. I find hellebores among the most beautiful flowers of all, so try to grow as many as possible. Hellebores are available in an enormous variety of shades and markings, all of which press very successfully indeed, but none more so than the plum-coloured *Helleborus atrorubens*. There are several other winter flowers, such as snowdrops and similar bulbs, that can also be pressed with pleasing results, so you might consider keeping a particular area of your garden solely for winter

pressing. It need not be a large bed, but just a suitable corner, not too far from the house (you must bear in mind the possible weather conditions) and with reasonably dry access. The flower bed can then be augmented with annuals later in the year when the bulbs are over.

You will see from the table listing flowers suitable for pressing (*see pp. 14–15*) that there is a wide variety of flowers available during the summer months. Perhaps you could then use your small winter corner as an experimental area, planting out any new specimens not mentioned in the table that you think might have pressing potential. You will have to be ruthless if you find that they don't press successfully, and either move them to another site in the garden, or give them to someone else.

Another interesting way to fill a flower bed is to think of a colour scheme and plant out accordingly. Since it is just as important to press foliage as it is flowers if you want to create realistic pressed pictures, you should carefully consider what sort of foliage to grow. Grey and silver are definitely the most successful colours when pressing. Virtually every plant that has grey leaves will press well (apart from the ones that are too fat in the leaf), so you will have to decide which shapes and shades appeal to you the most. For example, there are dozens of varieties of artemisia which are extremely successful in the press.

Grey and silver foliage plants grow in every shape and size, from the thistle family that can tower above everything else, to the very small alpine plants with silver leaves that can be extremely useful for miniature work. My favourite grey plant, both before and after pressing, is *Alchemilla alpina*. Under the mid-green leaves of *Alchemilla alpina* is a beautiful shimmery silver effect which you can see in several of the photographs in this book. This plant is well worth hunting out – a specialist nursery would probably order it for you.

If you would like to plant a silvery grey

bed but want to add some flowers as well, you can keep to the silvery theme by adding pale and dark blues, creams and whites, all of which blend with the grey to give a stunning overall effect. We have all become used to matching colours in the home, and perhaps a little colour co-ordination in the garden would not go amiss. The very words used to describe a beautiful garden – 'a riot of colour' – suggests that beauty is not necessarily regimented or politely colour co-ordinated. However, single or limited colour schemes can be very lovely and a popular addition to the garden.

Left: *A clump of* Helleborus atrorubens *growing in a wood.* Below: *A silver foliage border, featuring* Santolina senecio, *achillea and* Stachys lanata.

CONTAINER GARDENING

So far I have only referred to gardens, perhaps even inferring gardens of a reasonable size. However, one really does not need extremely large amounts of space to grow the flowers needed for this very enjoyable hobby. Obviously if your growing space is limited to a window sill you will not be able to grow some of the larger plants, but you could specialise instead in miniature work.

Naturally, your choice of pressing plants will be determined by the growing area at your disposal. However, if that space is very limited you may find it worthwhile only growing the plants that are not easily available from florists. You will then increase the number of different specimens that you can press.

A window box is more than capable of

supplying you with some of the flowers you may want to press, and you can buy other flowers from a florist to supplement what you grow yourself. With luck, you may know people who will let you have flowers and foliage from their gardens too.

There is also the option of using wild flowers, although that is only feasible if you live in or near the country, and you must be very careful about which flowers you pick – some of them are protected species. There are many wild flowers that can be legally picked, but always ensure that you only

Below: *Even without a garden, there are still many plants that can be grown in a window box to give plenty of scope for pressing.* Right: *This stone tub is not only a decorative feature but is also the perfect site for plants.*

choose large and flourishing plants, and never, ever, remove the plant completely by its roots. So many people visit the countryside and pick wild flowers because they find them pretty, only to have those flowers wilt and die long before they can be arranged in a vase. Therefore, if you decide to pick some common wild flowers that are not protected by law, take your press with you into the country so that the flowers and leaves can be pressed immediately.

If you are planning to plant out a window box, carefully read the lists of flowers and foliage that can be pressed successfully (*see pp. 12–19*) to see which ones appeal to you, and also which plants are suitable for the size of container you will be using. Large plants, such as old-fashioned roses, may be out of the question, but you could consider

miniature roses instead, and there are many alpine plants that could be ideal.

There are several foliage plants that thrive in a window box, given the correct amount of loving care – such as watering them regularly! Many of the herbs included in the list are of an ideal size, and any plants you don't press can be put to excellent use in the kitchen. Even if the herb will eventually outgrow its container, you can still plant it when young, press its foliage and then, when it becomes too large, pass it on to a culinary-minded friend who has more space. Among the other plants that are not only suitable for planting in window boxes but also pressing are many of the variegated ivies, some grey foliage plants such as cineraria, *Pyrethrum ptarmiflorum*, heathers and also miniature conifers.

To make the best use of the limited space in a window box, you can fit many small flowering plants between the larger clumps of foliage. Snowdrops, hyacinths, lily of the valley, pansies, miniature roses, lobelia, alyssum, forget-me-nots, common daisies or one of the small potentillas are all ideal candidates. So, as you can see, there is no need to be discouraged from growing plants for pressing even if you do only have a window box.

Even with just a small balcony, a few steps or a tiny patio, your choice of containers is considerably enlarged, thereby increasing the amount of plants you can grow for pressing. Tubs, urns, hanging baskets and even old butler sinks all make ideal containers for flowers and foliage.

If you suffer from a real lack of space, you can grow plants in grow-bags placed on window sills, or in minute patio or terrace gardens. For example, if you have a patio garden that is mainly paved, a few tubs can look extremely attractive, and you'll be able to pick the flowers as well as enjoy them as garden ornaments.

Raised beds are another attractive feature that can be used in patio or terrace gardens. Not only are they very much simpler to weed and maintain, but if you have a back problem they are easier to reach than if they are closer to the ground.

Facing page: *Violas and pansies turn this tiny stone bed into a colourful focal point.* Below: *Even if your gardening space is confined to a grow-bag, you should still be able to cultivate a number of plants.*

PLANNING A PARTICULAR TYPE OF GARDEN

One of the reasons for writing so much about growing your own plants is that not all flowers and foliage suitable for pressing are available from florists, which can considerably limit the palette of colours from which you will work. It is therefore considerably cheaper to grow the plants yourself. Packets of seeds are much less expensive than florists' flowers in the long run, but they do cost a lot more in time and effort. You must therefore consider your priorities, plus the amount of available space. If you have a large garden I would recommend that you try growing many of the varieties suggested in the tables of flowers and foliage (*see pp. 12–19*). If space is at a premium, you should decide which, if any, plants you wish to grow yourself and then rely on your florist, or generous friends, for all the other varieties.

If there is plenty of space in your garden, and you have an equal amount of spare time at your disposal, it would be marvellous to allocate a large area of your garden solely to growing flowers for pressing. If you like roses, you could consider planting a specialised rose garden. There are many hundreds of sizes, shapes and shades of rose, some scented and others not, some that will flower all summer long, and others that will only bloom for two or three weeks during early summer.

When planning a rose garden, it is important to consider the size and shape, height and breadth, scents and ultimate uses for the roses. For example, if some of the roses will be perfumed, then ideally they should be placed near the path, so that you can smell the scent as you walk past and, if you wish to bury your nose in the flower, you won't have to trample halfway over the flower bed to reach the appropriate bloom. It seems common sense to place the taller varieties at the back of

Devoting a section of your garden to a particular type of plant can be very effective and attractive indeed, as seen here in this collection of shrub roses.

the beds, or in the middle if they are to be seen from all angles, but other points can also be taken into account. You could try mixing the colours so that the roses look like a planted flower arrangement when they are in full bloom.

There are many varieties of rose that press well. The modern shrub roses, or single roses, are by far the most consistently successful, and are much easier to use once they are pressed. All hybrid teas and the majority of the floribunda roses have to be dismantled petal by petal if you want a really good end result, and then re-assembled for use in the pressed flower picture.

An important point to bear in mind when choosing roses for pressing – or any other flowers, for that matter – is that once anything has been flattened it appears much larger than when it is viewed three dimensionally. Therefore, some of the larger single roses become giant-sized once they are pressed, and can really only be used for big arrangements on walls, such as murals, so try to concentrate on the smaller varieties of rose, as you will still be astonished at their relative size once they are pressed.

The new breeds of patio roses, Polyantha roses, and the modern shrub roses mentioned above, are all excellent subjects for pressing as they are considerably smaller than some other varieties, and bear a constant flow of flowers throughout the summer. In this regard, they are much better value as plants than such species roses as *Rosa xanthina* 'Canary Bird' and *Rosa moyesii*, both of which only flower for a couple of weeks during the early summer. If this flowering season coincides with a period of terrible weather, you could lose the entire crop for that year.

Whatever the size of land or terrace you have at your disposal, a little lateral thinking will prove that there are always ways and means of providing yourself with enough plant material to experiment with the very enjoyable pastime of pressing flowers.

CHAPTER THREE

BUYING FLOWERS FROM THE FLORIST

*There are many suitable flowers and pieces of
foliage that can be obtained from florists. Supplies
are now available from all over the world, thereby
extending their seasons and meaning that many
flowers are on sale almost all year round.*

Florists' Flowers and Leaves Suitable for Pressing

FLOWERS	METHOD	COMMENTS
Alchemilla	Presses	
Alstroemeria	Books	Heavily marked only
Asparagus fern	Books	
Carnations	Books	Petals only, preferably dark-edged
Conifer	Heavy press	
Daffodils	Books	Cut in half
Delphiniums	Books	Blue/white
Eucalyptus	Heavy press	Small shoots
Freesia	Books/presses	
Gypsophila	Presses	
Heather	Heavy press	White and pink
House plants	Presses	Non-succulent

FLOWERS	METHOD	COMMENTS
Ivies	Presses	Variegated
Larkspur	Presses	All colours
Lily of the valley	Presses	
Mimosa	Heavy press	Preferably in bud
Orchids	Books	Beware – not easy
Other ferns	Books	Dainty plants
Roses	Books	Petals only, any colour
Skeletonised leaves	Books	Any
Tiger lilies	Books	Cut in half
Tulips	Books	Dwarf ones only

BUYING FLOWERS
FROM THE FLORIST

As you will see from the table of flowers available from florists (*see pp. 32–3*), there is a large number of possibilities on sale at your local florist. You therefore have no excuse, even if you have no garden facilities at all, not to experiment with flower pressing!

Very often florists' flowers are received in the form of bouquets or presentation arrangements, and one is always very reluctant to press immediately some of the flowers that have so kindly been sent. While I am not suggesting that you immediately dismantle an arrangement of flowers, perhaps after a day or two you could carefully remove a leaf or two, and a few flowers. It won't look quite as the florist intended, but you will have a lasting reminder of the lovely gift once the flowers have been pressed.

In the case of a bouquet, it is much simpler to remove some of its contents before you arrange the flowers in a container. In that way, the flowers will be at their best for pressing, and you will still be able to enjoy some of the bouquet as fresh flowers. Sadly, not many of us are often the lucky recipients of bouquets and presentation arrangements, so here are some tips on pressing flowers bought singly or in bunches from a florist.

When buying flowers for pressing from a florist, remember that you will need far less material than you would to create an arrangement of fresh flowers. A good example of this is a rose: in order to press it successfully, you have to dismantle it petal by petal, and when you are re-assembling it you really only need half the amount of petals, so you can create two roses from one original flower. Also bear in mind that if you want to make some authentic-looking rose buds, each one will only need three or four petals, so several buds can be made from one flower. Therefore, there is no need to buy large quantities of expensive flowers to make a lovely picture. The essence of an attractive picture is the quality of the pressing and design rather than the amount of flowers and leaves. With pressed flowers, it is very much a case of quality rather than quantity.

Having said that you need not buy large quantities of any one flower, do remember that you are bound to have a certain percentage of failures in your press, no matter how hard you try. Flowers and leaves, being natural materials, have a mind of their own and regardless of how carefully you follow my instructions on how to press, some of the petals will decide to bend before the press is shut, or develop brown patches for no reason at all. So always buy more flowers and foliage than you think you will need to allow for some spares.

It is always a good idea to make friends with your florist, as not only will they then know your requirements, but you will also discover on which days they attend their local flower market, or receive wholesale deliveries, and therefore when their flowers are at their freshest. Think of buying flowers in the same way as you would buying fish: always look for fresh, unmarked blooms. It is a waste not only of your valuable time but also of your press space to work with cheap flowers that are obviously past their best. If you put sub-standard flowers into the press, I can assure you that very sub-standard flowers will come out. Many people seem to think that they can press any old rubbish, but actually the reverse is true – only very high-quality flowers will give a successful finish. Another point to remember is that flowers will wilt badly, or even die, if they are left sitting in a hot car or office all day, so if you have to buy them hours before they will be pressed, put them in plenty of water as soon as possible or, better still, buy them on your way home and then they can be pressed fairly quickly.

Immediately pressing a few flowers from this bouquet will ensure that they are preserved while in top condition, and mean that the remaining flowers can be enjoyed in a colourful arrangement.

CHAPTER FOUR

HOW TO PRESS SUCCESSFULLY

No matter how great one's design ability, or how beautiful or costly the materials with which you frame your design, if the pressed flowers are not perfect then you will be wasting both time and money. This chapter therefore describes the techniques you will need to follow to obtain perfect pressed flowers.

FLOWER PRESSING EQUIPMENT

There is no need whatsoever to spend large amounts of money on flower pressing equipment, since the majority of items are either very inexpensive or are things you may already have around the house.

Without doubt, the main item of equipment is the flower press itself. Presses are easily obtained from a great many shops and are not very expensive, although if you wish you can make your own, or ask a handy friend to help out if you are not very practical. To make a press like the ones shown in the picture on the facing page, you will need two pieces of plywood approximately 20cm (8in) square. It is up to you whether you choose to leave the wood in its natural state, or stain and varnish it – either way you will not affect the performance of the press, simply make it look more attractive. The press in the bottom left of the picture has been finished and the one in the top right has not. To make the presses look even more attractive, I have laminated a flower design on to them, but this is purely a matter of choice and taste.

Having obtained your two pieces of wood, place them one on top of the other, ensuring that they are exactly square, and tape or clamp them securely together. You will then need to drill a hole in each of the four corners, about 13mm (½in) in from each side, using a drill bit that is slightly larger than the diameter of the four bolts you intend to use. These bolts should be about 7.5cm (3in) long so that you can fit several layers of blotting paper, newspaper and flowers into the press. There is no need to go to extremes and choose bolts that are about 15cm (6in) long as they will be very unwieldy and can cause considerable problems when you want to carry the presses about. Finally, you need four wing nuts and washers to hold the bolts firm when you tighten the press.

Having made the basic press, you will need to cut out some blotting paper and newspaper or corrugated card to fit – I would recommend cutting out enough paper to give ten layers to a press. Many people suggest using corrugated card for pressing and indeed, most commercially made presses are supplied with corrugated card, but I have always had enormous difficulty when using this, finding that it leaves the imprints of stripes on the flowers and leaves. However, this is purely a matter of experimentation and discovering what best suits your method of working. The corrugated card does allow air to circulate through the press, which is very helpful, but nevertheless I prefer to place fairly thick wads of newspaper between the sheets of blotting paper.

The basic pressing technique is rather like making a sandwich. First cut the newspaper and blotting paper to fit the shape of the press, and then arrange the flowers to be pressed on a sheet of blotting paper laid on top of a layer of newspaper. Cover the flowers with a second sheet of blotting paper, and then another layer of newspaper, before beginning another layer of blotting paper and then one of flowers. Continue assembling the layers in this order. You will therefore need eleven small wads of newspaper and twenty pieces of blotting paper in order to fill your press with ten layers of flowers.

The following will all come in useful but with experience you may find alternatives that suit you better.

Equipment checklist

2 pieces of 20-cm (8-in) square plywood
4 7.5-cm (3-in) bolts
4 wing nuts to fit the bolts
4 washers
11 pads of newspaper, each approx 10 sheets thick, cut to fit the press
20 sheets of blotting paper, cut to fit the press

Fine to medium paintbrushes are useful for moving flowers and leaves around, and for brushing hairs and fluff off

the design once you have finished it. They can also be used for applying the egg white, if that is the method you decide to use.

Tweezers are a crucial piece of equipment and should be used at all times to handle the pressed material. Flowers are very brittle once pressed and if you try to touch them with your fingers they will be completely ruined, no matter how careful you are. There are several types of tweezer on the market, so experiment with different lengths and shapes to see which suits you best. I would recommend first trying a pair of tweezers that are intended for stamp collectors, as these have slightly rounded ends, are longer than normal and can be far easier to use.

Craft knives can be useful for trimming pieces of pressed material if they are too large or the wrong shape. I use a very small one that looks like a pencil or pen.

Perspex rulers are invaluable. An 18-cm (6-in) ruler is not only used for its measuring abilities when framing designs, but also if you are working directly on to a

This photograph shows a collection of presses and flower pressing equipment.

piece of material rather than card, it is easy to slip the ruler under the fabric when you sign your picture.

Adhesives can be either rubber solution glue or egg white, which was used by the Victorians, and I think it is still the best option as it does not mark the leaves and flowers – commercial glues do after a time. However, egg white is not the easiest adhesive to use at first and you may prefer to use a rubber solution glue.

Glass cleaners are essential for cleaning the glass of finished pictures, so choose whichever brand you prefer. You will also need a good selection of cloths for cleaning the pictures – pieces of linen work well, as do old T-shirts. However, do make sure that you choose fabrics that don't leave tiny specks of lint on the glass. Finally, keep some pieces of tissue or rag nearby so that you can wipe your hands should they become covered in glue, egg white, or both!

PREPARING THE MATERIAL

Apart from the press that you will have either bought or made, you will also need a supply of heavy books, telephone directories and more blotting paper when pressing flowers. There are several ways of pressing plant material and, generally speaking, the lighter the material involved, the lighter the weight needed to press it successfully.

For example, when pressing individual rose petals, they need only the lightest pressure and give the most successful result when arranged between sheets of blotting paper which are then placed inside a telephone directory. Allow about five folded pieces of blotting paper to one directory, spacing them equally so that the pages of the directory act like the newspaper in the press. Two or three directories should then be piled on top of each other, followed by a couple of books (not containing any flowers) to act as weights. If you press rose petals too heavily they are quite useless, losing their colour and becoming transparent.

However, before you place any flowers into presses or books they will have to be properly prepared. This is because a complete rose is not usually ready to be pressed in one go, so you must condition it first by stripping it of its leaves and thorns, cutting the stem and then crushing it with a hammer, before placing it in fairly deep water. This will keep the rose fresh while you carefully remove the outer petals as the flower gradually opens. If you try to press petals from a rose that is still closed, the petals nearest the centre will be so tightly curled that they won't press into a good shape, and you will have wasted your rose. Instead, take two or three days to press all the flower, each time only placing the outer petals in the telephone directories as the rose gently opens.

Do not neglect any part of the plant being pressed, because you can usually find some use for it. If you are pressing roses, for instance, make sure you press some of the green sepals as well, as these are very useful when compiling pictures later on.

The smaller leaves on the roses can also be pressed, of course, but you will have to discard the stalks as their thickness prevents them being pressed successfully. When pressing freesias you can use almost all the flower, as well as some of the stem. Separate the individual flowers since, as they are trumpet-shaped, they can either be pressed whole or cut in half: this gives a variety of colour and thickness. Also press the small sprays of buds at the tip of the stem, thinning out any buds that are too thick and bulky.

Never place items of differing thicknesses on the same sheet of blotting paper. For example, the freesia buds are quite thick and, if they were placed in the same layer as the petals, they would prevent the thin flowers from receiving even pressure from the weight above. So, place all the flowers in one layer and the thicker buds or pieces of stalk in another.

Remember that the amount of care and time that you take in pressing your material will be very apparent when you look at your finished work, so never be tempted to cut corners. Shapes that are easy to use can also be created at this stage. For example, you can form a curve in a stalk by positioning it in the required shape and then securing it with tiny pieces of tape for the first couple of days of pressing. After this you must remember to remove the tape so that the entire stalk can dry out. Think about the shape of the flowers that you are pressing and try to place the blotting paper on top of them as carefully as possible to ensure that they will lie flat under the weights, because once they are permanently pressed you cannot start again.

The tables given earlier in the book (*see pp. 12–19*) recommend various ways of pressing the flowers and foliage mentioned. However, you are bound to discover for yourself many species that I have not had space to describe, as it is always interesting to experiment for yourself. As a basic rule, it is useless trying to press any plant, such

as a succulent, that contains a large amount of water, but nearly every other type of material can be attempted. This is because the more water held by the petals of a flower, the greater the chance that it will dramatically change colour once pressed. In the case of orchids, nearly all of them turn dark brown or black. This makes it difficult to incorporate them into a colour scheme, although a well-pressed orchid can look very effective as the centrepiece of a design if surrounded by flowers of complementary colours.

Top: *These roses have been placed in a pot of water prior to being pressed gradually as the petals open.* Below: *Whole freesia flowers should be arranged on a sheet of blotting paper before being pressed in a book.*

PRESSING TECHNIQUES

Once you have pressed some standard plants that definitely give good results and are confident with your pressing techniques, I strongly recommend that you start experimenting by pressing all sorts of flowers and foliage. If you begin your pressing experience the other way round you may be disappointed or dismayed by any unsuccessful results. In some cases I have deliberately not mentioned a particular plant because I consider it to be unsuitable for pressing, but I am sure that there are many plants not listed that will press very well.

A good rule is to look at the shape and size of the flower before you press it, and then imagine what it will look like once it is flat. Most of the bell-shaped flowers are much harder to press, as they do not look as pretty when viewed in two dimensions as they do in three. Many flowers that are very popular favourites in the garden are of little use to the presser. I have tried pressing several beautiful tulips but once they are pressed flat they become very large indeed! Some pressed tulips can measure as much as 20cm (8in) in diameter, which makes it very hard to use them unless you are planning an enormous picture.

When pressing flowers with fairly hard centres, such as Christmas roses, it is easier to remove the middles completely and either discard or press them separately and replace them later. If you have discarded them, you can use false centres when assembling your design, such as a floret of cow parsley or the centre from a

potentilla or daisy.

It is always wise to examine a flower very carefully before placing it in the blotting paper as if it contains any tiny insects they will think they are being provided with a picnic lunch and eat their way through the contents of your press!

As I have just mentioned, the requisite time for pressing most materials is between six to eight weeks. The process can be speeded up somewhat by changing the blotting paper several times while the flowers are being pressed, although you must be extremely careful as the plants will be exceptionally fragile at this point and it may do more harm than good to disturb them. Ideally, you should pick clean, dry and perfect specimens and then control your impatience by leaving them

undisturbed for six weeks before you discover how well they are pressing.

Ideally, flowers should be picked for pressing between 10am and midday, as by this time the dew will have dried on the petals or leaves but the sun will not yet have faded the colours. Always pick a flower on the very day that it comes into full bloom, because the process of ageing takes place very rapidly in flowers, and pressing does not rejuvenate them, but only halts the ageing process at the moment of pressing. So, for the best colours and such details as

Below: *The hard centres of such flowers as hellebores should be pressed separately for the best results.* Facing page: *As well as pressing lily of the valley flowers individually, you can also press them in small sprays.*

bright yellow stamens, the flower must be picked as it is coming into bloom. The cardinal rule is to avoid thinking that you can press such flowers as overblown roses that have already lost half their petals. You wouldn't make a special cake as a present with long out-of-date flour and stale eggs so don't think that any old ingredients will do for making a pressed flower picture.

Labelling is another very important point to remember. Every time you put some plant material in a book or press, you must have an efficient way of knowing the date on which you pressed those particular items, so that you know when to remove them. Otherwise you may take flowers or foliage out of the press before they are ready, thereby ruining them. Obviously it can also be essential for you to know what flower or leaf you have pressed, although you will discover that on examining the finished material. Masking tape is an excellent way of marking things, because it usually peels off without damaging the paper to which it was fixed, and makes a clear, creamy coloured background on which you can write the date. If you wish you can add a few details about the particular plant and perhaps even where it was collected. Nothing is more infuriating than, six weeks later, taking out some really beautiful specimens from the press and not being able to remember which friend's garden or which field you found them in. Although it may be too late to gather any more that season, you would at least have a permanent record so you could return in the following year to collect some more.

Flower pressing is not one of those crafts that abounds in short cuts, for it requires a very painstaking and patient approach. Rushing through it will result in failure, and very disappointing that can be, too. The most reliable way to press anything is always to dismantle it completely. For example, to prepare lilies of the valley for pressing, you must remove each bell and press it individually. You can then press a few sprays from the top of the stem or,

It is important to store pressed material flat, away from direct sunlight and as free from dust as possible. This small chest of drawers is an ideal container.

alternatively, press the entire empty stem, encouraging it to bend in a pleasing curve, and then re-assemble the bells on to the stem when you come to use it in a design. Although this may seem a very tedious way to go about things, it is the only sure method of success. I cannot think of any flower that does not press better for being taken apart, although of course you will have to spend time putting it back together again when you want to use it. A great deal depends on the level that you wish to achieve: I believe that only the highest standard is worth aiming for, but your patience may dictate otherwise. So, for perfect results, reduce everything to the lowest common denominator before putting it into the press.

If, for some reason, you have to press some flowers that are not completely dry (and you should only do so in an emergency), then you must first mop them with some clean paper tissues to soak up any droplets of water. Ensure the flowers are as dry as possible before placing them on the blotting paper, as any remaining moisture will encourage mildew to form and spoil all your efforts.

Leaves are much hardier and will stand any amount of bad treatment, but having said that don't try pressing damaged or nibbled leaves in the hope that they will look better once they have been pressed because they won't! However, as a very occasional desperation measure if a flower or leaf is useless because it has inadvertently been creased or folded, I have been known to try pressing it with an iron on the lowest setting. I don't advocate this as a standard pressing technique, but if a flower or piece of foliage is already damaged you will have nothing to lose in trying to iron it. Autumn leaves don't mind this sort of treatment, but you will have to be extremely careful when handling pressed flowers. Place the problem item between two sheets of blotting paper, then gently iron over them. In some cases it will not help at all, and the flower will turn brown, but sometimes you will find that your problem has been solved and you have a perfect flower or leaf once more.

Once the six to eight weeks of pressing time have elapsed, you can inspect the material to see whether it is completely dry or not. If so, it will be fairly rigid and slightly brittle. Don't try to remove anything before it is ready as it will only go wrong in the long run, making all your work so far a complete waste of effort. Instead, control your impatience and wait for another week or so before testing the material again. Placing the books or presses in an airing cupboard will speed up the pressing process slightly without damaging the flowers.

When the moment has finally arrived that your specimens are ready for use, you will have to devise a way of storing them safely. Of course, they must be kept flat and if any pressed material is left lying around uncovered it will begin to curl up. There are several possible storage methods, so choose the one that suits you best. The most elementary way is to leave the material on its original sheets of blotting paper, piling them up on top of each other. The major drawback to this method is that it can be very time-consuming sorting through the piles when you start a new picture. Also, blotting paper is fairly costly to buy so it is much more economical to use it for pressing time and time again.

The most effective method that I can recommend is to remove carefully all your pressed flowers and leaves from the blotting paper with a pair of tweezers, and store them in small, clear-fronted cellophane bags. You can then quickly identify the contents of each packet, determining the shade, size and species. Overfilling the bags is a false economy as you will swiftly ruin the contents, making them bent, crushed or torn. So, only fill each bag with enough material to lie completely flat, and don't mix colours or types of flowers or foliage in the same bag.

Finally, you will need to find a suitable storage container for the bags, to enable them to lie flat, keep them out of direct sunlight and free of dust. Small metal filing cabinets intended for stationery, little plastic tool cabinets or shallow trays made from card are all suitable receptacles, and you will easily find other ideas to suit your needs. Sort out your material once you have amassed a reasonable collection, perhaps grading everything by size and colour, and separating the leaves from the flowers. In this way you will quickly be able to find the pressed material you want when you begin designing a picture.

Before you re-use the newspaper and blotting paper for another batch of plant material, do ensure that it is thoroughly ironed to remove any moisture, or you will affect future pressings. You should also inspect the paper for any signs of mildew and throw away any sheets that are affected before they transfer the problem to the next collection of flowers and foliage.

CHAPTER FIVE

FRAMING THE PICTURE

After ensuring the quality of your pressed flowers and foliage, the next priority is to check that the standard of materials with which you will surround your picture is equally high. The type of frame that you choose can either make or mar your work.

The Importance of Frames

The type of frame you choose for your finished work is an entirely personal decision, based on your own likes and dislikes, but I would strongly suggest that you think about the type of frame you will be using right from the start of your work.

If you are uncertain of the type of frame you want to use, or even of the very important role it plays in setting off the finished picture, browsing through the photographs in this book should give you a good idea of the tremendous versatility of frames, and also show you how the correct frame will focus the eye on the design itself, as well as balance all its elements.

Very often, finding an unusual frame can spark off an idea for an equally unusual picture, and I cannot stress too highly the need for a beautifully made frame to give a professional finish to your work, as a cheap or shoddy frame does absolutely nothing to enhance the picture whatsoever. Think of this craft as an art form – if you had painted a really good watercolour you wouldn't nip down to your local chainstore and buy a very basic and somewhat unattractive frame for your work of art. Instead, you should honour your work with the type of lovely frame that it deserves.

There are dozens of points to be taken into account when choosing a frame – with what style of room it must blend in, and what personal choice the recipient would make (it is, of course, easier if the picture is intended for yourself). There are heavy frames, light dainty frames, expensive frames and inexpensive but still attractive ones, as well as older styles or very modern designs.

The first decision – and I am assuming that you are choosing the frame before the pressed flower design has been created – is to decide what shape of picture you want. There are round frames, ovals that are thin or more rounded, fuller ovals, rectangles, squares, hexagonals or very long, thin panels. In some cases it helps to imagine the place where the picture will be hung, although this information is not always available, particularly if the picture is intended as a present.

Oval frames, such as the ones shown in the photograph on the facing page, are a very popular choice for many people but they are usually considerably more expensive than square or rectangular frames. You can buy oval frames made from plastic, but they are usually not very well finished and will not do a lot to improve your design, or wood, which in my opinion is always worth paying a little extra for.

There is a very wide variety of finishes available, such as gilded or silvered, and with or without a highlighting gold line, as well as the enormous range of woods themselves, which vary tremendously in colour and atmosphere, and can be inlaid with veneers or kept quite plain. In addition, there are metal frames made from silver, brass or gilt.

When using an oval frame it is not always necessary to use a mount, and an oval shape can suggest several attractive designs. For example, it lends itself to a curve following the outline of the frame, a garland or a solid design.

Square and rectangular frames are usually made from 2-m (7-ft) lengths of moulding, which are then cut down to size. If you are making your choice at a picture framer's, you will be given samples of the woods and finishes from which to choose. These are usually presented as small corners made up in the particular moulding to give you an idea of the finished effect, but any reputable framer will be able to answer any questions you have, as well as give you plenty of sound advice should you need it. For example, some woods turn darker as they age, so you may want to take that into account when choosing something very pale.

This selection of oval and round picture frames shows the enormous variety that is available, ranging from very simple gilt and wooden frames to more intricate designs combining paint and gilt.

RESTORING OLD FRAMES

You can derive an enormous amount of satisfaction from restoring old frames and returning them to their former glory, and it is astonishing the number of attractive frames that are discarded when someone changes the colour scheme of their home or sorts through their attic and throws out something that is battered but still beautiful.

If you wish to use old frames for your pressed flower work, you may find just what you are looking for at home, or by rummaging around in junk shops or at auctions. However, very often the frame looks rather tatty and in definite need of some loving care before it can do proper justice to your work.

Your intended frame may have a broken mitre, or a missing section of decorative moulding. The gold covering may be flaking away, exposing the white plaster, or gesso, underneath. If the frame appears to be in reasonably good condition, you may find that you work wonders by just giving it a proper clean. To do this, use some soft cotton wool, dipped in white spirit, to remove any ingrained dirt, repeating the process several times if necessary until you have dislodged and removed the years of neglect. Polishing with a soft cloth will bring the surface back to life.

If any pieces of gold leaf have been chipped off to reveal the white base, there are various shades of gilt waxes which can be rubbed on with a soft cloth and then buffed up to a fine lustre. If you are unsure of which to choose, take the frame with you to a good art shop and ask an assistant for some help. It can be extremely difficult to memorise colours correctly, and you may be very disappointed to realise that the shade of gilt wax that you thought was a perfect match in the shop actually bears no resemblance to the colour of the frame. Gold paint never gives a satisfactory finish, as it rarely matches the beautiful patina of old gilding, which in turn helps to distinguish the genuine article from a reproduction.

If the frame is a particularly good one with relatively little damage, it may be worth repairing the problem areas with gold leaf. Seek professional advice if needs be, rather than make a valiant attempt yourself and then regret it.

Broken or missing sections of moulding can be restored using dental plaster. Alternatively, and especially if the damage is extensive, you can use a rubber mould material to make an impression of a piece of moulding that matches the missing section. Make a cast of this with a suitable filler, remove it from the mould when set, and clean it with a file and glasspaper until it matches the original moulding. The piece can then be glued on to the damaged area and made ready to receive the gold leaf.

Gilding – the laying of gold leaf on to surfaces – requires a great deal of patience and practice to achieve a good result. The surface to be worked on must first be given several coats of gesso, a mixture of rabbit skin glue and whiting. Once dry, each coat must be rubbed down with very fine glasspaper to give a surface that is as smooth as possible. Any flaws in the surface will show through the gilding. A thin cream called red bole is then painted over the gesso to provide a rich base on which to lay the leaf. The area to be covered is then dampened with a very diluted solution of rabbit skin glue, before the gold leaf is carefully positioned and laid down. The surplus leaf is then dusted off with cotton wool prior to burnishing.

All this, of course, is a very simplified description of an extremely old craft that has largely disappeared. This is because the time and preparation needed to achieve the perfect finish cannot compete with the sophistication of modern moulding manufacturing processes, which have improved the standard of mass-produced leafing while keeping the cost of the finished mouldings at a realistic level.

Restoring old frames can call for specialist help, but nevertheless there are several techniques that can be practised at home.

CHOOSING A FRAME

When choosing a frame, one of the most important considerations is the style of picture you wish to make. If you choose a very rough and heavy frame, the picture should have a rural atmosphere (*see p. 83*), but if you choose an elegant and formal frame the picture will also have to be formal (*see p. 113*). Try holding a heavy frame and then a delicate one around a piece of card or photograph, and you will see the difference in effect, and be able to make your choice accordingly.

The choice of finish is again mainly linked to the room or style with which the picture will match. If the pressed flower picture is to hang in a kitchen, then perhaps a pine frame would be suitable, or a frame with a coloured line that blends with the soft furnishings. On the other hand, a picture destined for a drawing or sitting room might look better with a gold frame or a wooden

one that complements the room. If there are already several pictures in the room, you could give them all the same style of frame.

There are several extremely elaborate mouldings available that may not appeal to everyone's taste (*see p. 73 and p. 115*). For instance, there are many with different colours of inlaid veneers and marquetry, and others that show beautiful hand-painted effects. Finding a special moulding can be a real inspiration for a picture and really boost one's enthusiasm, so spending some time searching for the perfect frame, or one that is very unusual, can be highly profitable.

Above: *These square and rectangular frames offer a good selection of different materials and effects.* Facing page: *Here are just some of the woods, bevels and finishes available from picture framers.*

MAKING A SIMPLE FRAME

Having decided on the type and style of framing for your picture, you must make sure that you buy the right materials if you are going to make the frame yourself. Most art shops offer a wide selection of mounting card in a variety of colours and thicknesses. Remember that the thicker the board, the wider the bevel of the cut. However, thick board can become rather difficult to cut through, and six-sheet board is a good average thickness with which to work.

Plain and simple mouldings can be bought at most timber yards and home decorating shops. However, if you want more variety and better value, there are many framers who can provide a comprehensive selection of good wood mouldings at a much cheaper price. Glass can be bought in ready-cut sizes, or in larger stock sheets that are less costly but have to be cut to size. The necessary tools for making a picture frame are a mitre box, a tenon saw, a hand drill, a pin hammer, a pair of pliers and a mitre clamp or vice.

1 The mitre box is U-shaped to accommodate the moulding, and has 45° guide slots in both sides through which the tenon saw is worked when cutting the moulding. Hold the moulding firmly against the far side of the mitre box with one hand and then hold the saw in the other hand and draw it diagonally across the moulding to cut the mitre. When the length of one side has been marked out on the moulding, again position the moulding in the mitre box and with the saw now travelling in the opposite guide slots, make a further mitre cut to complete one side. Use this side as a guide to mark up the measurements on the opposite side, before cutting, and then repeat the process for the other two sides.

2 When the four sides have been cut, usually giving two short sides and two long ones, you must join together a short side with one that is long. To do this, apply some wood glue to the faces to be joined and, using the mitre clamp to hold the two pieces of moulding exactly at right angles, drill

guide holes in the corner of the mitre and hammer home some pins to secure the joint while the glue sets. At this stage, you can use glasspaper to smooth the joint, and work the wood dust into the glue of the mitre to fill any slight gaps. Repeat this process on all four sides to make up the complete frame.

3 If a window mount is to be used around the picture, you must cut a thick mounting card marginally smaller than the inside measurement of the frame. Faintly mark the position of the window on the face of the board, possibly using slight pin holes to indicate the corners of the window. With a steel rule held firmly in position to guide a heavy-duty craft knife which is held at an angle, make a clean, bevelled cut between the pin holes to create the window. Mount cutting is a skilled job, so it is advisable to practise on some offcuts of mounting board before attempting to cut the real thing.

Cutting the glass is simply a matter of scoring it to the required size with a glass cutter. Then, with a T-square positioned under the score mark, apply firm pressure to snap the glass. This is a very simple operation if you have the correct tools and a little confidence, but it can be a nightmare to the learner. Do practise on offcuts before cutting a larger sheet. It is a great help to use a good tungsten-tipped wheel cutter, as it will stay sharp for a long time and pay for its slightly higher cost with better cutting.

Finally, you must cut out the backing. This can be made from 2-mm ($\frac{1}{12}$-in) hardboard, and is either cut out with a saw or with a heavy-duty craft knife. Hanging accessories, known as 'D' rings, are best fixed to the hardboard with rivets, which are secured by pushing through the ring and then through a hole made in the hardboard, before being split open with a hammer. 'D' rings are flat, and much stronger than the unattractive eyelets that so many framers screw into the sides of frames. Nylon cord, rather than wire, is the best choice when hanging the picture, as it is extremely strong and hard-wearing.

CHAPTER SIX

CHOOSING THE RIGHT BACKGROUND

At this stage, you can enhance or detract from a design according to your choice of background colour. The chosen shade may lift the picture and make it look more attractive or ruin it totally by clashing or overpowering the design itself.

CHOOSING COLOURS AND BACKINGS

Once you have chosen a suitable frame and you know which pressed flowers are at your disposal, you must now make a definite decision about the exact colour scheme of your design by choosing the backing for the picture itself.

There is an unlimited number of ideas from which you can choose to back your picture, using any fabric from a dainty piece of real silk through tweeds, rough and raw silks and linens, to hessians, velvets, cottons and even several layers or pieces of different materials. You could choose a plain dark colour and cover it with a pale piece of lace, or even make a patchwork background on which to place your flowers. This is where the innate artist in you gets the chance to come to the fore. You can copy other people's ideas and follow their suggestions, but ultimately the real satisfaction comes from designing your own colour scheme and knowing that the entire creation is yours alone.

You can spend hours browsing through shops looking at different fabrics, but as well as considering rolls of material don't forget to sort through remnants. These are an obvious choice since you are unlikely to need more than ½m (1½ft) of fabric, at the most, to back your design. Although it is fun to browse and choose whatever fabric appeals to you the most, there should be some definite planning behind your purchase.

First, you must decide on the sort of atmosphere that you wish to give your picture. Is it to be an up-to-the-minute design that will look good hanging in a bedroom or up the stairs, or should it have an antique feel to match a similarly styled sitting room? Not all materials are suitable for both modern and period treatments – for example, a dark velvet usually looks best in an antique-style frame, whereas a pale pink silk or cotton can be an attractive choice for a more modern setting.

Once they are pressed, the majority of flowers belong to the middle range of tones because of the colour changes that frequently take place during pressing. It is usually much more successful to choose either a very pale background that contrasts with medium to dark colours, or a very dark background that sets off very pale and silvery grey shades. If you choose a backing in the middle of the tonal range, such as a bright turquoise green, its colour will be so strong that it overpowers those of the pressed materials. If you look at the pressed flower pictures in this book you will see that I have chosen backing materials that contrast with or complement the colours of the flowers.

Patterned fabrics may appeal to you, but they should be treated with the utmost caution. It is very difficult to design a pressed flower picture on to a background material that has already been printed with a design, and if you were to use a floral fabric it might be hard to spot where your picture stops and the print begins. You can work with very subtle self-patterned fabrics, and pieces of lace can be very successful, but once again you should avoid choosing anything with too striking a pattern. Textures in the fabric can be a very useful addition, and materials such as crushed velvet, hessian and tweed all give a particular character to the picture and can work very well. Obviously you would be ill-advised to choose a very dainty gold oval to frame a background of rough hessian or sacking, and you could be very disappointed if you were hoping that a pretty pale blue crushed velvet would create a country-style effect.

Depending on the shape of the frame that you have chosen, you may also wish to use a mount in the picture. This means you have two choices to make – not only a suitable colour for the mounting card but also the background to go with it. If you feel this makes your first attempts at pressed flower pictures rather too complicated, you can begin working with a simple picture arranged on a plain cream card and make your designs more ambitious each time.

Mounts can add a great deal to your

picture, and there are many different sizes and shapes from which to choose. You may be happiest asking a professional to cut out your mount unless you are confident that you will do it properly, as it is a skill that takes a long time to perfect, and a badly cut mount is as off-putting as a badly made frame. There are several different examples of mounts in this book: one unusual mount is cut in the shape of an archway (*see p. 119*); a narrow gold line has been drawn around a rectangular pink mount to complement the aperture (*see p. 85*); and there is one design using four apertures in one mount (*see p. 141*).

Mount card is available in a wide variety of colours and textures: you can buy linen finish board and marbelised paper mounts, plain clear colours and soft, almost tweedy shades. Beware of matching too many colours together – if you have chosen a fairly strong coloured mount then it may be easier to have a plain white or cream silk as the background, or you could use a plain mount card in a neutral shade like cream, behind the coloured mount of your choice.

This photograph shows the contrast between modern and traditional frames, with appropriate backing fabrics and mounts.

CHOOSING FABRICS, FRAMES AND PAPERS

Whether you have chosen card or material as a backing for your mount it must be something that blends well with both the frame and the mount, not to mention the flowers.

The fabrics illustrated in the two photographs here are all natural colours, because they complement the soft shades of the pressed flowers. Dayglo orange, pink or lime green would never make a successful scheme, although having said that, everyone's taste is different! Just as most people co-ordinate the colours of their clothes, so you will achieve the best results by colour co-ordinating your pictures. If you want to use some very bright red flowers, choose a subtle, gentle background with which they can blend. All the shades of the same colour spectrum blend together well: for example, if you have selected a walnut or mahogany finished frame and you want to use flowers in shades of orange, cream and yellow, then a mid-brown mount with a beige or cream backing would tone very well with your design. Another example would be a picture made up of shades of grey, when you could accompany a grey or silver frame with a pale mount, perhaps

dove grey in colour, with a dark charcoal backing which would show off all the silvery grey leaves and white flowers in the design.

Many woods are strongly coloured, so take the shades of your wooden frame into account when you are considering what colour scheme to use. It's no use just thinking that you have a wood frame at home – take it with you to the framer's so you can match the actual colour of the wood. The range of woods is enormous, from dark mahoganies, through maples that can be almost bright orange, to a natural pine or bleached wood effect that can be very light indeed. For instance, if you have chosen a lovely maple frame, with its attractive grain, it would not blend well with a pale pink background – a brown or gold colour scheme would be far better. The exception to the rule is white or cream, since they usually go with anything and everything. Naturally, the brighter the white, the more it will suit pictures with a modern style, so consider choosing at least

Facing page: A selection of blue and pink fabrics for backings. Below: Some backing fabrics in autumnal shades.

an off-white, if not a cream, for pictures with an antique flavour. However, as a general rule you cannot go wrong with the basic colours, and if you are in any doubt don't try to use a complicated mix of colours and textures. Instead, keep your background uncluttered, for it's the simple pictures that often work the best.

Although most people are aware of the tremendous selection of fabrics on the market, not everyone knows of the vast range of papers that are currently available. Forsake your usual stationer, who probably won't have the room or the reason for stocking unusual papers or cards, and go to a specialist art or paper shop instead.

Apart from a large range of marbled papers sold in many different colours and tones, there are also papers that are made from plant material themselves, and so would be very interesting to use in a design. Most plant papers are made in Japan, using nettles, ferns, grasses or seeds, in all sorts of shades and styles.

Generally speaking, but not necessarily, including the rarer Japanese papers, card or paper can be a lot cheaper to use than fabric, especially since the majority of pressed flower pictures do not need large amounts of backing. Even a picture measuring 30 × 25cm (12 × 10in), which is large enough to display quite a few flowers and takes a fair amount of skill, would only need a backing 30cm (12in) square, so ½m (½yd) of material could be enough for about eight pictures, depending on the width of the material. A sheet of card can be far cheaper, and the more expensive papers are often available in small pieces.

Because papers and cards do not move about, and also accept adhesives easily, they are much easier to work on than fabric, and so are perfect for beginners, as well as anyone looking for different and unusual effects.

The variety of colours and textures of paper available is astonishing, and there are even some that look like lace.

CHAPTER SEVEN

WORKING OUT THE DESIGN

This is the most enjoyable part of pressed flower craft, but it can also be the most daunting. In this chapter I show you how to create some of the basic design shapes used to make pressed flower pictures. Once you are confident of the basic techniques, your imagination can take over.

ASSEMBLING A DESIGN
STEP BY STEP

The photographs shown here illustrate the four basic steps taken in building up a design.

1 Starting first with the leaves, arrange them into a basic C-shape. They need to be visible all the way round, so leave a space for the flowers in the middle of the design. When you are working on curved designs you should try to sort through your material and choose stems that are curved, as they will give a much more natural effect than if you have to use entirely straight pieces and encourage them to curl. In a design of this kind, where the flowers and leaves are built up in layers, you should try to look at the outline that will be visible (in this case, the outer leaves), and make sure that they are lying at pleasing angles.

2 Once you have placed the leaves in position you can then add some fillers or feathery pieces to soften the outline. In the example shown here, I used blackberry leaves, with *Statice latifolium*, or sea lavender, to make the outline more dainty, as its lovely grey-green colour blends in well with the pale green of the mount. This was cut from a piece of linen texture board and then backed with some cream silk. When you have established the base on which the flowers will be laid you can then start to arrange the larger flowers.

3 The position and arrangement of the bigger flowers will be determined by their variety and colour. Here, however, I first arranged the four large mauvey purple hellebores, and then the dark red single roses, *Rosa moyesii*. Once these had made a balanced C-shape, I then filled in any remaining gaps with some hybrid musk roses 'Ballerina', which are a lovely shade of pink and are very useful flowers.

4 To give the all-important finishing touches to the picture, I added several yellow potentillas, and some potentilla centres to the hellebores, as the middles had been removed when they were pressed. At this stage, it is a good idea to cover the picture with glass and leave it for a while. When you return you will be able to view your work much more objectively and see whether there are any glaring holes or flowers in the wrong place.

I use this basic method of building up the design on a bed of leaves, as it gives a good three-dimensional effect, but there are several other ways to achieve an equally pleasing design. For instance, you can build up a design that looks as though it has been pressed as a single spray (*see pp. 98–9*), although in fact each flower and leaf should be positioned with care to give a natural effect. Many people prefer to create a

pressed flower design where the component parts do not overlap each other, and certainly this can give a flatter effect, but not one that I find as interesting. Once you have become used to handling the pressed material you will find many more ways of creating designs. Although this book can give you ideas, general hints and tips on how to press and arrange flowers, it is not until you really start designing pictures for yourself that you will have mastered the skill needed for this craft.

To avoid sitting in front of a blank piece of card and wondering what to do, you should plan your design in advance. Having chosen your frame, and then the card or material for the backing, you will have already made some important decisions about the picture you intend to create. Prepare all the following pieces that you will need:

Frame
Hardboard back to fit frame
Glass for frame
Piece of foam cut to size to pad the
   backing
Piece of card or fabric cut to size
Mount if you are using one
Glue, tweezers and other equipment

If you have decided to use a mount, the card or fabric should be cut slightly smaller than the mount and then taped to it securely. In the case of fabric, make sure that it is stretched fairly tightly across the mount to avoid any wrinkles or creases appearing.

First place the hardboard on the working surface, then the foam, followed by the fabric, card or mounted backing, and then put the glass in a safe but accessible place.

In choosing your background materials you will already have made a commitment to a particular colour. For instance, if you have chosen colours that are suitable for a pink picture, you should pick out all the flowers that you have in shades of pink, and perhaps white as a contrast, plus some green or grey leaves, or a combination of the two, and some small feathery pieces to soften the outline. Once you have made your choice you should put the rest away out of sight, as they will only muddle you and make the job a lot more difficult. Work from the example and stages shown here, and be very disciplined about the number of flowers you use in each picture. I like a picture to be fairly full as if it is too empty it can become boring to look at after a few months, but it is very easy to get carried away with all your lovely pressed flowers and try to fit them all into one picture – using too many flowers looks just as bad as not using enough. Perhaps if you promise pictures to several friends and relations, that will help you to be a little more sparing with your collection of pressed material!

FIXED DESIGNS

Now comes the part that calls for real concentration and a steady hand – applying the glue or adhesive. This holds the pressed plant material in place, allowing you to build up a design without dislodging any of the flowers you have already arranged.

First choose whether to use egg white, which is the traditional adhesive for pressed flowers, or some modern rubber solution glue. If you want to use egg white, which is definitely the superior method, then separate an egg, pour the egg white into a cup and lightly beat with a fork until it resembles a thin sauce. It can now be applied with a small paintbrush.

Always choose a brush that is in good condition, and pull out any stray hairs before beginning to apply the adhesive. I find that bristle brushes are the best. If you are working with a rubber solution glue, you will find it easiest to apply it using a large clean pin or a piece of wire, about 6.75cm (2½in) long.

Whether you are using glue or egg white, the adhesive is always applied in the same manner. Carefully lift each piece of leaf or flower used in the design and apply a smallish amount of glue to its underside. Take great care not to apply too much adhesive as it will show through or seep out once the glass is pressed on to the picture. Allow the adhesive to dry for a couple of minutes, then gently try to move one or two pieces, checking to see whether they have been stuck down firmly enough. If everything seems to have been fixed in place try tilting the picture at a slight angle to see if anything seems to be slipping. However, don't move the design around too enthusiastically in case you dislodge any unattached flowers completely.

If you are satisfied that you have glued everything well, you can then proceed with the framing as set out in the next chapter.

When fixing a design in place with egg white or glue, avoid getting the adhesive all over the picture as it will catch the light when dry.

MAKING MATCHING DESIGNS

An important consideration to bear in mind when planning any design is whether you want a single picture, a matching pair or even a set of three or four, because your decision will influence the way in which you create the picture.

The photograph on the facing page shows a pair of pictures, illustrating two curved designs bending round towards each other. In this particular pair of designs, I have used matching leaves and similar tones for the flowers, although you could create two designs that are very different and link them together with matching frames or mounts. If planning a set of three pictures, you could arrange the flowers in curves for the two outer pictures, and create a solid design for the middle one (*see p. 81*). This type of arrangement looks extremely effective going up (or down) a staircase.

In the picture on the left hand side of the photograph, I used silverweed leaves, white alyssum, roses and larkspur leaves. The other picture also has silverweed leaves, with forget-me-nots, potentillas, hydrangeas and daisies.

There are two ways of arranging the designs, either working on each one at the same time, or completing one before moving on to the other. However, if you are just beginning your pressed flower work, you may become extremely confused when working on the two pictures simultaneously, so I would recommend that you work on one design at a time. Otherwise, you could find that you get the piles of pressed material confused, and end up with two pictures that are very similar rather than two individual designs.

Arranging pressed flower pictures in a small group is usually a great success, as the contents of the designs will all complement each other. You can create many different patterns, such as hanging an oval picture between two rectangular pictures. Another effective combination is square and circular pictures, perhaps with one of the square pictures above its fellow, and a circular picture either side. The combinations are endless, but you will get the best results if you choose the pattern you wish to make with the pictures before starting work. The pictures can then be made as a set right from the beginning, rather than just hanging together three or four pictures that you have already made, in the hope that they will be complementary. Another approach is to decide on a colour theme, perhaps to co-ordinate with the room in which the pictures will hang. If you are making the set of pictures as a gift, you should consider the favourite colours of the recipient or perhaps choose shades that blend with a colour scheme in their home. After all, there seems to be no point in spending many hours carefully making someone a set of pink designs if that is the one colour they can't abide!

For example, if your theme is pink, you could choose a pink silk background and no mount for one picture, have a pink mount with a cream silk backing for another picture, choose a cream card with a pink wash line around the aperture and pink paper behind the mount for a third, and perhaps create a fourth with a plain cream satin background. Then you could blend all these different backings together by choosing the same frame for them all, but perhaps in different sizes or shapes. This would give you four separate pictures that together form a set, linked by the same frames and the colour pink.

It is only with practise and experimentation that you will discover which shapes you most enjoy creating, and which designs work best for you. You may find, for example, that curved designs are much easier to create than solid ideas, or vice versa. Try to think of your own original shapes as well, as these may be far more appealing to you than any suggestions I have made in this book.

The use of different flowers for each picture means that each design stands on its own but when the pictures are placed together it is obvious that they form a pair.

MAKING A CURVED DESIGN

For many people, this is one of the easiest shapes to create, so it is a good design to choose when beginning your work with pressed flowers. When creating a curved shape always try to use as many naturally curved pieces of plant material as possible – their shapes will help to accentuate the mood and rhythm of your design, as well as add continuity.

Obviously the curve can face either to the left or the right, and after a little experimentation you will find which sort of curve is easiest for you to create. This will be largely determined by whether you are right- or left-handed. You can also adapt this design by turning it round to make a landscape design, so that the curve resembles a flattened horseshoe.

For the design photographed on the facing page, I chose the frame first because I was so attracted by its marble effect and the inlay banding around the frame. The grey mount was chosen to blend with the grey marbled effect of the frame, but I deliberately kept it plain to accentuate the frame's veneer. A more complicated mount might have distracted one's eye from the flowers and the frame. I then put a cream silk backing on the mount, again to keep the overall effect as plain as possible, since I planned to design a fairly full flower combination in the oval aperture.

The majority of the flowers and leaves in the design were chosen for their tones of silver and grey, but I added a few silvery pink flowers to give some additional colour and interest to the design. I used silverweed leaves, with a few pieces of sea lavender, or statice, tucked in between them. Having created the basic shape, I used some *Anemone japonica* flowers, but positioned them upside down to make the most of their silvery appearance, plus some *Alchemilla alpina* leaves, also upside down. Having arranged all the larger flowers in the design, I then filled it out with some astrantia and potentilla flowers.

The soft tones of the colour range always produce a successful design and the joy of using all the silvery tones is that they last so well. In many cases, the silver-grey effect is created by the very small hairs on the underside of the flower or leaf, which catch the light and give a lovely overall tone to the picture. It can be equally successful to use ranges of blues with silver (*see p. 117*), and whites and creams always blend well with the lighter coloured leaves.

Try to avoid using any one component in a design that is much darker than all the others. If you have chosen a flower that is very dark and striking, make sure that at least one of the other flowers has the same colour value. Otherwise, one's eye will be drawn to the darkest flower or leaf in the picture, which will act as a distraction from the overall shape and impact of the picture. Similarly, you must be very careful in your use of the brightest and lightest colours. A subtle blend of golden yellows, reds and browns can be spoilt by using a really overpowering bright orange flower right in the middle of the design. It would be much better to use several bright orange and bright yellow flowers, plus some strong-coloured leaves, to make a very striking and vivid picture. If you use brilliant white flowers, such as larkspur or some of the daisies, you must ensure that there are several light tones in the picture, otherwise one's eye will automatically focus on the white flowers and only then fall back on to the rest of the picture.

So, for a curved design you can work solely with more subtle colours or, if you prefer the brighter and more vivid shades, use several of them in the picture for balance. In that way you will either have a subtle blend of colours that is always pleasing to look at, or a bright cheerful picture that shows off all the flowers.

The basic curve is a good design with which to experiment, and many flowers and leaves curve naturally. If you want to create a C-shape but all your pressed material curves in the opposite direction you may have to let the flowers and foliage dictate the design.

MAKING A
SYMMETRICAL DESIGN

The pleasure of a design like this lies in its symmetry, and the way in which the flowers are arranged. When planning such a design, you must always imagine that a vertical dotted line is running down the middle of the picture, so that the flowers and leaves must be the same on either side of it. You can also imagine a horizontal line bisecting the design, so that in effect the picture can be divided into four quarters, all exactly the same. Having spent years ensuring that mounts are cut accurately, and working with the straight lines of frames, I find straight lines just as pleasing in designs as curves, and I think an idea like this makes a pleasant change from the more popular floral compositions.

I chose a frame in a fairly plain wood and finished in a medium oak colour. This is because it reminded me of the type of frame one might put around a tapestry or sampler, and I feel this symmetrical design is somewhat reminiscent of sampler work and needlework in general. Having chosen the frame, I wanted a plain light background that would clearly show off the design, so I used a fairly heavy cream fabric – very often I avoid white backgrounds as the contrast with the flowers is too stark and harsh. Once I had set up my basic ingredients, I then started working with the group at the bottom of the picture. I positioned the rose first and then tucked a rose leaf either side of it. To lengthen these shapes, I placed two more leaves at each end of the group, and then softened the design by adding some small sprigs of alchemilla.

Once I was pleased with the bottom group I copied it, as a mirror image, at the top of the picture. I then turned the picture round and completed the other two sides. Once the fourth side was completed, I positioned the central rose and its leaves, then found suitable, slightly smaller, roses for the four corner groups. Obviously, as this pattern is made from natural materials, one cannot achieve the precision and effect of an exact replica that is obtained with a ruler and hand-drawn lines or circles.

However, the effect is just as attractive, and perhaps the beauty of the design is actually enhanced by the slight discrepancies in the shapes of leaves and flowers.

There are many possible variations on the theme of symmetry. You could draw an imaginary diagonal line across your design and match the resulting two triangles, or you could have more than one aperture cut into a mount and create a symmetrical design to fill each one. For example, working with a rectangular picture, perhaps 32.5 × 17.5cm (13 × 7in) and allowing 2.5cm (1in) all the way round the apertures, you could create two 12.5-cm (5-in) square apertures next to each other. You could then fill the left-hand square with a design and create a mirror image of the design in the right-hand square. This idea works well using such designs as L-shapes, placed back to back to resemble book ends.

Another idea that uses a mirror image is to make a pair of pictures, either in separate frames or housed in the same mount, in which the colours of the flowers and foliage are transposed. For instance, you could use leaves in tones of golden brown and orange, with flowers in shades of cream, pale green and silver, for one picture, then reverse the colours in the other picture so that the foliage is in the pale shades and the flowers are orange and golden brown. It can be great fun creating designs like these, and they look very effective once they are finished. Obviously you will encounter some limitations, as there are not as many different-coloured leaves as there are flowers. You could always cheat a little and use skeletonised leaves for a cream colouring, though if you look carefully through your collection of pressed materials you may find quite a few unusual shades. When pressed, *Clematis montana* leaves and tendrils turn almost black, as do some orchids, and several autumn leaves, including Japanese maple, become burgundy. Several plants have yellow leaves and very new eucalyptus leaves can look blue, so your scope may be much larger than you imagine.

Another interesting idea is to create a silhouette picture. For instance, if you use a plain cream background you can create a design entirely in black, perhaps using *Clematis montana* leaves. Young elder tree and ash tree leaves can also turn black sometimes once they have been pressed. Elderflower buds become black if they are pressed when still green, and you could use these, or *Clematis montana* tendrils to fill in the design. Amongst the flowers that turn a very dark colour when pressed are deep red primulas and auriculas, as well as small orchids. When designing a silhouette picture you will have to adopt a different technique from normal, as the shape of the flowers and foliage must really stand out against the background. Try to keep any overlapping to a minimum so that the outlines of all the plant material used are shown to their very best advantage.

The inspiration for this picture came from a colouring book of my daughter's, which contained a selection of patterns and designs, some of which were symmetrical. I thought this idea might work well if transposed to pressed flowers.

MAKING A LONG AND NARROW DESIGN

The clean lines of rectangular-shaped frames lend themselves to elegant and sophisticated designs, so try to bear that in mind when planning a picture such as this. Long and narrow shaped pictures can be very useful if you want to fill an awkward space in your home, such as the area between two doors or in a small alcove.

When assembling the design, place the leaves in position first. Thinking of them as numbers on a tall, thin clockface may be useful, so first put a large leaf into the twelve o'clock position and then one at six o'clock. Position smaller leaves at three and six o'clock, then continue in this way around the clockface until you have made a bed of leaves. Add some softer leaf shapes if necessary, then begin to position the flowers. Once again, start with the largest flowers and place one at the top and one at the bottom of the design, and then two staggered in the middle. Complete the design by tucking in smaller flowers to fill in any gaps.

In the photograph shown on the facing page, I used some silverweed and thalictrum leaves, as the long thin leaf shape of the silverweed contrasts nicely with the smaller dainty groups of thalictrum. The flowers in this design include the patio rose 'Gentle Touch', the modern shrub rose 'Marjorie Fair', some larkspur and a few potentilla ('Miss Willmott').

The colours used are a selection of lovely soft greens and pinks. When I originally found the frame I thought how pretty it would look if the green of the surround was carried through to the mount and the colour of the picture. I also liked the antique effect caused by the crackles in the gold. The pale green mount was chosen to blend with the many different shades of leaves and flowers that I had in store, and is made from a linen textured mountboard which gives a more interesting effect than plain green card. The cream silk backing seemed an obvious choice as it blended with the cream of the frame and helped to keep the colour combination very gentle.

As a general point when choosing colours to blend with your backgrounds, it is very much easier to make a successful combination of soft colours than harsh ones. Gentle pastels such as this light green, or a soft light pink or blue, are much kinder to the eye and don't detract from the overall design. Having said that, many of my favourite pictures have been really bold designs using very strong colours on striking backgrounds! An example of the stunning effectiveness of this colour combination can be seen in my design using a very dark background and the brightest red roses that I could find (*see p. 6*). If you are new to making pressed flower pictures, it could be easier to work with some pastels and then experiment with brighter colours once you feel more confident about your design skills.

The versatility of rectangular-shaped frames means that you can make pictures that vary considerably in size, from the very small to the size pictured opposite, which is 30 × 15cm (12 × 6in). Of course, you can make extremely dramatic pictures that are much larger than this – I have made many lovely pictures with frames that are about 65 × 25cm (26 × 10in), which can be used with or without a mount. It is a lot easier to work on a firm card background, such as a pale cream mount card, when making pictures this big. That is because the stiffness of the card helps to control the increased amount of pressed material being used.

As well as creating a design like the one pictured here, you can use the long narrow shape to create an elongated twisting design, rather like a string of entwined S's, or a natural piece of vine creeping along the frame. Once you begin to experiment you could be inspired into creating a whole host of ideas for long and narrow designs.

Long and narrow frames make the perfect setting for such sophisticated pressed flower designs as this one.

Making the Wreath or Garland Design

This design was inspired by a trip to New England, in the United States, where placing garlands of dried flowers on front doors is a traditional sign of welcome. Once I got home I translated the idea into a pressed flower design. A picture like this would make a marvellous gift for someone moving into their new home, as it would continue the theme of welcome.

I have used some very strong colours in this design, and especially the burgundy-toned mount. As the red roses remain such a vivid shade after pressing I think they balance the colour of the mount beautifully. The plain cream silk was a fairly easy choice for the background of the picture, as the introduction of another colour would have been too confusing and would have spoilt the balance of the picture.

Starting with the leaves, I mixed both green and silver for the outside of the circle and used some medium-sized wild rose leaves and medium-to-small silverweed leaves, placed alternately around the edge. I then filled in a little with some alchemilla flower sprays and some very pretty reddish-grey fronds of grass which I found growing on our compost heap!

Then, arranging the largest red roses at equally spaced intervals around the circle, I balanced them with the large single pink roses – it is always important to introduce both light and shade into a design, otherwise it can look very dull. The smaller red roses were positioned next, not only to emphasise the overall burgundy theme but also to introduce various sizes and shades for interest. By this stage the circular shape was building well, but I needed some smaller flowers to fill out the edges of the wreath, so used some *Anemone japonica* to balance the dark reds. I added a few small hydrangea florets to perfect the shape and add some depth to the range of colours used. Hydrangea florets can be picked and pressed in the autumn when they are a lovely green shade with reddish tinges, although you may have to choose your bush carefully as they do not all have the same density of colour.

Don't feel restricted to a circle if you want to make a garland design, as it can easily be manoeuvred into other shapes. An oval-shaped wreath can look very effective if it follows the lines of its oval frame, and you can make a similar style of garland in a heart-shaped design, whether small (*see p. 85*) or much bigger and bolder and enclosed in a square frame. Another attractive idea is to make a square or rectangular garland that follows the shape of its frame.

Calligraphy blends very well with pressed flowers and introduces many other ideas for design. One very effective idea is to write a short poem on an attractive background and then arrange some pressed flowers around it or to one side. Another successful design of mine was to surround a harvest poem with harvest-time leaves and flowers forming a decorative border. You could use this idea for any season of the year, either copying a poem you know or making up your own: a poem written by a friend or loved one can be a much treasured gift. If calligraphy is not a skill you possess or think you could learn, do not despair for there are some alternatives. You could use some of the dry transfer lettering that is available from most art shops, or ask your local framer or photographer if they could recommend a calligrapher to you.

Another gift that was well received was a book of poetry for which I made a pressed flower bookmark. I chose my favourite poem in the book and wrote one verse on the accompanying card, and then decorated it with pressed flowers to match the bookmark. There are so many possibilities for pressed flowers that I hope you find it hard to contain your enthusiasm!

When choosing the frame for this design I looked for something that would show off the dark red colours of the flowers and also be fairly plain, so as to balance the rather busy design. In some places the reddish undercoat of the frame shows through the gold moulding, echoing the reds in the picture.

MAKING A SOLID DESIGN

I have deliberately placed this design idea at least halfway through this chapter as I feel, despite looking quite easy, it is in fact one of the more difficult designs to perfect. There is a limit to the size of picture that you can create in this shape, as a solid mass of flowers can lose all sense of size or identity when it becomes too large. I once attempted to make an oval three or four times as large as the one shown in the facing photograph, but it was an abysmal failure, so I wouldn't recommend it. Although you can scale up the size and shape of the leaves and flowers, the huge numbers that have to be used to fill the picture mean that the overall effect is lost, and you cannot appreciate the beauty of each flower as there are so many of them.

For the design shown here, I used an oval frame measuring 25 × 20cm (10 × 8in), which is a very useful size as it looks good in both large and small rooms, and can be particularly pretty in a bedroom. I used a medium-brown velvet background and chose all the contents of the picture to blend accordingly. The leaves are a large cultivated thalictrum, as opposed to the wild variety (see p. 77). The brown fern used between the thalictrum leaves came from the bottom of my previous garden, but any brown fern would be suitable. In many cases green ferns, and particularly bracken, can darken during pressing, or you can deliberately look for ferns that have already changed colour. I then added a few alchemilla leaves to provide a contrast with the dark background.

When working with the flowers, I first arranged some large yellow roses at regular intervals around the picture and then positioned the peachy-coloured roses. The gaps were then filled with hydrangeas and potentillas. It is difficult to advise on getting the correct balance of this particular design, because it is partly a case of trial and error. Nevertheless, try to ensure that the flowers do not end up arranged in straight lines, as this can look like a stripe in the design. It also helps to vary the shapes of the flowers as well as their colours: for example, hydrangeas are much more pointed in shape than roses, and the petals of potentillas are widely spaced and so give a more pronounced petal shape.

It is much easier to create this design with contrasting colours overlapping each other to show off the shapes of the flowers. However, I have made some very unusual designs in which very little colour was involved at all, and sometimes I have used only cream, beige, white and the occasional touch of grey to make solid designs that rely on texture rather than colour. When working on such designs, it is important to choose a background with as much texture as possible, and a fairly substantial frame to set off the design.

Although pressed flowers are basically only two-dimensional because they have been flattened, it is quite possible to use several of the thicker ones to build up a good three-dimensional effect. For instance, many grasses remain much thicker than most pressed flowers, and very interesting pictures can be created with different layers and textures, perhaps only with leaves and grasses, and therefore with no need for flowers.

You must take care when mixing thick materials and the more dainty, thin, petals, as the thicker grasses can prevent the glass coming into contact with the flowers, so that they eventually curl up. In the same way, if you place thin flower petals on top of any lumpy plant material, its uneven shape can damage or crease the petals, and so mar the finished result.

The individual shapes of the petals and foliage play an important role in this design. I deliberately chose the hydrangeas for their pointed petals, which made an interesting contrast to the very rounded shapes of the yellow potentillas and the roses. On the other hand, the spiky nature of the brown ferns was echoed by the slightly spear-shaped thalictrum leaves.

Making a Botanical or Natural Design

Usually when designing pictures I tend to use a particular leaf or flower because of its shape, colour or texture, and pay no attention to its species or variety. However, there is wide scope for creating designs with a botanical feel, and in the picture shown on the facing page, I decided to use the leaves and buds that were picked from the same plant as the main flowers, thus creating a design that was botanically correct.

In this particular case I used wild roses, plus their buds and leaves. The frame around them is extremely heavy, but I chose it because it reminded me of some of the heavier framed Victorian pictures that have a botanical feel. This picture frame moulding came complete with all the scratches, dents and marks that make it look old, although it was in fact new.

Generally speaking, natural designs like these need to be shown against fairly plain backgrounds, and particularly so in the colour sense. For instance, a background of turquoise card would not give the right feel to this picture at all. In the same way when choosing a frame, it is better to use a wooden or plain gold frame rather than a pastel colour or something that is heavily decorated. By their very nature, botanical-style pictures are a traditional subject and therefore look best when treated as such, with a traditional type of frame and backing.

The example shown here is not a traditional botanical picture, but more a natural spray or group. Another way of producing a picture that is botanically correct would be to choose a larger aperture (rectangular is probably the easiest shape to work with) and to show several pieces of the same plant. Wild flowers make excellent subjects for botanical pictures, as they can have some lovely shapes, but their colours are not as strong. Keep the vivid cultivated flowers for pictures in which their colour is an integral part of the design.

Having decided which plant you wish to place in your botanical picture, collect pieces during the year to show the changes in the plant throughout the seasons. For example, if you worked with a seed head, you could show a sample of the plant from a side view and another viewed from straight on, a stem and some leaves with a tiny piece of root attached to create a very attractive design, but only do this if the plant has been grown in your garden or in that of a friend.

Whenever you decide to pick some wild flowers – which is not an idea I concur with at the best of times – you must never, ever, remove part of the root as this reduces the size of the plant that other people could enjoy. In fact, if the sample of the root were taken carelessly it could damage, or even kill, the rest of the plant, and the countryside needs all the help it can get nowadays.

You can create a delightful design using wild flowers, with some pressed pieces of moss as a base (pick only tiny, very green, fronds of moss, and not great big muddy lumps). Positioning the moss at the bottom of the picture, push the wild flower stalks into the moss so that they seem to be growing naturally. Try to choose flowers that are quite little and dainty, as a smaller scale wild flower picture is always more successful, as it emphasises their delicate nature.

So, you can certainly get successful results from pressing wild flowers, but don't expect them to keep their colours as well as their cultivated counterparts. Instead, use them in designs that have a much lighter, airier feel.

If you are very keen to try pressing wild flowers, do go to the trouble of checking which species are protected and be strong-willed enough to leave them well alone. Better still, do not touch any plants growing wild but instead grow some in your garden, as you can then pick as many pieces from them as you like. Both the seeds and plants are available from specialist nurseries.

MAKING HEART AND
DIAMOND SHAPED DESIGNS

So far in this chapter, I have described some of the plainer basic shapes, for often it is the less complicated shapes that work better than a contrived design. However, there are several other designs that can make very attractive pictures, as you will see in the rest of the book.

The photograph on the facing page shows two new designs – a heart shape and a diamond. The little heart has been put in a square frame, as any other shape would leave too much background space around the heart that would have to be filled. The actual size of the heart design shown here is 12.5cm (5in) square. I used a textured cream fabric as a backing, to add a little interest, although if it had been too heavy it would have distracted one's eye from the heart pattern itself. The flowers are larkspur and hawthorn, and some alchemilla and small rose leaves were also used.

There are many times when a heart-shaped design can be ideal – for example, you could make a Valentine's Day card with some very small red roses and their leaves, plus a small amount of asparagus fern to soften the outlines. Another suggestion is to make a wedding card, with the names of the bride and groom written inside a heart-shaped wreath of pressed flowers. One of my favourite photograph frames that I have made over the years is a 15-cm (6-in) square piece of card, into the centre of which a heart-shape aperture is cut about 7.5cm (3in) high. Around this heart-shaped cut-out I arranged a delicate garland of small apple blossom flowers and buds – as the pressed buds are a much darker colour than the flowers they make a good contrast. I fitted this into a narrow, plain gold frame, making a lovely present for a young girl or baby.

The diamond design shown in the opposite photograph is really an adaptation of the solid design (*see pp. 80–1*), although in this case you have to make a very definite outline with the leaves and then ensure that it is echoed in the shape that the flowers make in the centre of the design. In this example, I have used grey leaves from *Pyrethrum ptarmiflorum*, some herb Robert leaves, forget-me-nots, roses and Japanese anemones. This shape would work in either a rectangular frame, as in this case, or a square diamond would fit into a square mount, although it would have to be shorter rather than the elongated shape I have used here. The mount is particularly attractive in this example, with the pink card edged with a narrow gold line and the mount backed with cream fabric – the plain gold frame goes well with the gold line in the mount.

Other ideas include horseshoes, which are adaptations of the curve (*see pp. 72–3*) and would be ideal if you wanted to make a card or picture for a wedding or twenty-first birthday. You could fill the centre of the design with a special message if you wished. Another special design shape is the spray (*see pp. 114–5*), and if you wanted one that was lighter in feel, you could create a spray of flowers with the stalks still showing as though they were an unwrapped bouquet, or a spray made to look as though it was a sprig from a bush or tree, with some flowers intertwined with the leaves.

Another, more complicated, idea is to make a picture resembling a vase of flowers. To do this, cut out the outline of the vase or urn from a large leaf (an enormous autumn leaf is very useful as it has an interesting texture) using a craft knife, and use the shape to form the container at the base of the picture. Then arrange some flowers in the vase, remembering to position a few so that they overlap the top of the vase to soften as many hard lines as possible, with perhaps one or two leaves or flowers ranged around the base of the vase for a more natural effect. When done well this design can look exceptionally attractive, but when badly handled it can look very ugly, so practise with several vases before choosing which one to use, as subtlety is one of the key factors in the success of this picture.

A further shape that I have used successfully is that of a bow. Although it's not a shape that I would recommend for a large picture, it can look very attractive used to decorate cards and calendars. Basically, the shape of the bow is created from leaves, and in most cases the smaller leaves and component parts are easier to manipulate into these less natural designs. Having formed the outline to your satisfaction, you can then fill in the solid part with flowers in your chosen colour scheme.

All of these ideas can be used once you are able to confidently create the more basic shapes. It is much better to try a simpler design and to be thrilled with the results rather than try something more complicated and then feel despondent because it didn't work.

I chose this frame especially for its plain qualities, so as not to detract from the shape of the design, but there is a small gold line on the inside of the frame to highlight the picture.

MAKING AN INITIAL DESIGN

Continuing the theme of unusual shapes, a very popular present is a picture in the shape of an initial. In these days when everything you can imagine is personalised, why not create a personalised picture? In the photograph on the facing page I have designed an S-shape for Sheen, but it could just as easily have been a J for Joanna, or any of the other letters of the alphabet. The majority of the letters lend themselves to design shapes, the only problems occurring with such letters as E. If you want to make them really small, the shape will have to be worked in tiny flowers to accommodate all the different angles clearly and give the letter sufficient definition.

For this S-shape I used rose leaves to create the basic outline, added some blue larkspur and white hawthorn flowers, and then softened the shape with some sweet pea tendrils and small pieces of Russian vine. The blue theme was continued by using a pale blue-grey linen mount card backed with cream silk and surrounded by an attractive gold frame.

Of course, there are many different types of lettering that you can choose for your picture, ranging from something very angular, such as a plain capital A or an elaborate copperplate A, to a gothic-style A which would be even more elaborate.

You can choose between creating an upper or lower case letter, although the easiest shape of all must be a C, as it is exactly the same as the standard curved design (*see pp. 72–3*). Remember to make the shape of your mount echo that of the letter you are designing – for example, if you want to create a capital I, it will fit far better in a long, thin, rectangular mount, say 22.5 × 15cm (9 × 6in), with an aperture 5cm (2in) smaller all round, than a circular frame or mount. Also, try to introduce as much detail into the letters as possible – the example opposite looked very dull until the sweet pea tendrils and Russian vine had been added to give movement and interest to the design.

Another possibility that I have experimented with once or twice is creating a monogram in flowers. This has to be handled carefully if you are to ensure that you don't lose the shape of the letters you are trying to incorporate in your design. It is best to use small flowers and leaves and create a medium-to-large monogram, otherwise the picture can quickly become an unwieldy blob.

As well as letters, you could use the flowers to make numbers. Little girls love flowers just as much as big girls, and you can make an excellent birthday card for a child. For example, the number eight would be a very pretty shape to create and a pressed flower card reading eighteen or twenty-one could also be very attractive if created in shades of pink, and if you had the patience you could even make a matching gift tag to accompany the present.

Another possibility is to decorate the mount of a pressed flower picture with small groups of flowers, or to arrange a design on a plain backing with no mount, and then create the effect of photographic corners with single flowers and a couple of leaves, arranged about 2.5cm (1in) in from each corner of the frame. Alternatively, you could create a small design as though it were in a vase or a natural spray, and then surround it with an archway of flowers. This would then have no mount, but just a plainish frame, to avoid the overall effect seeming too cluttered. As you can see, there are a great many ideas that can be created, and you could even try making a flower rainbow. Every time you admire an attractive shape or see an article that you think could be decorated with flowers, jot it down in a special notebook so that you'll have plenty of inspirational ideas ready and waiting whenever you need them.

If you are unsure of which style of lettering to choose for an initial design, look through some magazines or books for inspiration, or browse through a catalogue of dry transfer lettering until you find a typeface you like.

CHAPTER EIGHT

FINISHING OFF THE PICTURE

This chapter shows you how to finish your picture once you have completed the design. There are also ideas for making the picture look even more effective and attractive when it is hung on the wall.

Finishing the Picture

Once you have completed your design, you must ensure that you cover it with a sheet of glass should you have to leave it at any time. This is because pressed flowers need to remain under pressure at all times, and if left uncovered for too long, they will begin to curl up, thereby ruining your picture. It is well worth covering your design with some glass and then carefully putting it to one side for a while before returning to it later. You may well find, on looking at it again, that there are various elements that you want to change, and it is much easier to take an objective view of your work if you are looking at it with a fresh eye.

Having decided that you are satisfied with the picture, it is then time to tackle an essential, but also rather tedious, part of pressed flower work – framing and finishing. It is extremely important at this stage to take unlimited amounts of time and trouble, as the success of your design will stand or fall by the way in which it is finished. Small bits and pieces straying under the glass, or fingerprints on the glass, can only detract from the finished result, no matter how attractive it is.

First, place your design in front of you, ensuring that you have an excellent source of light. If necessary, use an angle-poise lamp to ensure that every hair or piece of fluff has been spotted and then removed. Once the glass is fitted it will magnify any hairs that are on the backing material, and therefore ruin the picture.

Carefully study the entire design, check that you have glued everything in place properly, and then gently brush away any hairs, fluff or any other foreign bodies from the background and ensure that the picture itself is absolutely pristine. Then clean the piece of glass really thoroughly, first washing and then drying it, either with a proper glass cloth so that no pieces of lint are spread over the surface, or using a proprietary glass cleaning product and a suitable cloth.

Once you are satisfied that the glass is spotless, carefully place it over the top of the design. You must then perform a small conjuring trick – holding all the layers of the picture firmly together, turn the frame and picture upside down and place on the table, then fix on the hardboard back. There are several ways in which you can do this – I use a professional glazier's staple gun which is both quick and efficient, but if you find this too expensive an investment when you first begin pressed flower work you can use a hammer and nails instead.

Using a small hammer and 10-mm (3/8-in) nails, press down the hardboard at one end of the backing sheet and hammer a nail into the frame, then do the same at the other end of the sheet, to balance the pressure on the back. Each time pressing down very firmly on the backing sheet, hammer nails into the other two sides. You should then turn the picture over and check that there are no creases in the material, or marks on the mount or card, and that none of the plant material has slipped out of place. If you are happy with your progress so far, then continue to hammer more nails into the back, again exerting as much pressure as possible, until they are evenly spaced at intervals of about 4cm (1½in) or so around the frame. Alternatively, if you are not happy with your design, perhaps because some of it has come unglued or a crease has formed in the backing material, then you will have to remove the glass and rectify the problem before starting this process all over again.

If you are completely beaten by this painstaking stage of pressed flower work, then I suggest that you consult your local framer, who should be very helpful and be able to quickly produce the professional finish that you want. It is much better to admit defeat and carefully transport your design to an expert, rather than spoil it by not being able to frame it properly. Try to

The more exacting you are in putting the finishing touches to the picture, the better the result will be.

glue all the plant material really well if you think you may need help with the framing, as this will make the framer's job a great deal easier.

Once you have passed the framing stage the only job left for you to do is to finish the back and make it as airtight as possible, to prevent any damp reaching the pressed flower material. There are various ways in which you can finish a picture. For example, you can seal the gap between the hardboard and the frame with masking tape, but make sure that you do this as neatly as possible. If working on an oval picture you will have to use several small pieces so that they follow the shape of the frame (*see p. 91*). A much tidier, though more time-consuming, method of finishing the picture is to cover its entire back with paper, fabric or card. I

Below: *Satin or embroidered ribbons, brocades, bows and tassels can all give added dimension and interest to pictures.* Facing page: *I made this bow shape from a length of velvet ribbon before fixing it to the wall and the back of the oval frame.*

would suggest using paper, as this is the easiest option to apply, and there is a vast range of colours, and even textures, if you wish to extend your design skills on to the back of the picture as well!

Cut out the piece of paper, fabric or other backing material very slightly smaller than the back of the frame. Apply plenty of rubber solution adhesive to the back of the frame and hardboard, then carefully place the backing fabric in position, gently but firmly pressing it down all over the back and frame until it is evenly fixed.

Finally you must find a way to hang the picture. The simplest method is to use standard screw eyes, as shown opposite, or the more professional 'D' rings, and then, having fixed these screws about one-third of the way down each side of the frame, attach some nylon picture framing cord between the two. You can make do with string, but having spent so much time and care on creating a perfect picture, you might be somewhat annoyed if it fell to the floor and smashed because the string had broken! Then, turn the picture over and clean off any remaining fingerprints.

There are other accessories you can use to increase the impact of the picture, including cords, tassels and ribbons that could be added to pictures when they are hung on the wall. One very simple but effective idea is to hang the picture from a picture rail, or higher point, from a length of cord, rather than wire. Large or small ribbons can be attached to the picture or tied in large bows, and you can also buy embroidered ribbon to give a very attractive period finish to a picture.

A set of pictures can be hung from ribbons or cords – for example, a set of two or three miniature ovals can be hung down a length of ribbon, with a velvet or silk bow positioned at the top of the strip. In many cases when creating this effect, it is not enough just to tie a bow in a piece of ribbon, and you may have to actually create a bow from a piece of material in order to produce the right effect.

CHAPTER NINE

PRESSED FLOWER MINIATURES

Making miniatures from pressed flowers could really be an entire book in itself, as you need different and very particular skills if you are to be successful. In addition, you must be able to choose small flowers and small parts of flowers that can be used to good effect.

Choosing Suitable Small Flowers

The most important point to bear in mind when choosing suitable flowers for a miniature picture is their scale. As the photograph opposite shows, it would be quite impossible to include the large single roses in such a small picture, because the scale is completely wrong. Although this example takes the point to an extreme, I have noticed that many people mistakenly use flowers that are so big that there is barely room for them in the frame, and therefore the finished miniature is not as full of detail, nor as interesting, as a larger picture would be.

Scaling down your work in the way that is required for creating successful miniatures does not mean putting just one or two flowers in a smaller frame than usual. Instead, the very word 'miniature' means that everything should be of a smaller scale than usual, even including the fabric or card that you will use for the backing. For example, don't choose a raw silk with large slubs, or a handmade paper containing big flecks, as they will look enormous by the time they are enclosed in a tiny frame and will ruin the proportions of the picture.

The picture shown opposite is not a particularly small miniature – you can make really beautiful pictures using a frame as small as 2.5cm (1in) in diameter. However, what you should always remember is that the picture must contain a reasonable amount of detail if it is not to look dull. This picture has been placed inside a 7.5-cm (3-in) square aperture, and I used some small silverweed leaves, with a few sprays of forget-me-not, some geums, two pink larkspurs, plus several red and white hawthorn blossoms. Each time I chose the smallest flowers that I could find of each type – the larkspur flowers can range from this shape to nearly twice the size, so it will be worth while hunting through your collection of pressed items both to get some inspiration for your miniature and to determine your colour scheme.

Illustrated on page 95 is a pair of oval miniatures in silver frames. I chose a background of black silk to accentuate both the frames and the silvery effect of the designs themselves. The leaves are small sprays of silverweed, interspersed with little stems of forget-me-not. In the left-hand picture I used larkspurs and hydrangeas in shades of pink, with florets of cow parsley. I chose the same flowers for the right-hand picture, but used yellow shades instead.

This size of miniature looks quite lovely when ranged together in small groups of two or three, and I think they look best of all when hanging in a straight vertical line (*see p. 101*).

A large selection of miniature frames, and other small items suitable for pressed flower work, are available from craft shops. If, once you have begun working on miniatures, you find that this size of picture is more rewarding than larger items, there are dozens of other containers suitable for miniature pressed flower design. Careful searching through old junk shops and around antique markets may well produce endless ideas and inspiration from which you can work.

Victorian lockets look beautiful if they contain a tiny flower arrangement instead of a photograph, and if you are lucky enough to find a fob watch that no longer works you can transform it into a stunning and unusual frame for a miniature flower design. Even old brass curtain rings can be used as small circular frames, and I am sure that the more you look, the more the ideas that will come to mind.

Achieving the right balance in both the size and quantity of flowers and foliage in a miniature picture is extremely important. For instance, if you choose fairly large material you will be limited in the amount you can use and the resulting picture may look rather dull. If you find it difficult to track down suitably small flowers, looking through a book of alpine plants, or visiting a specialist nursery, could provide you with plenty of inspiration.

MAKING A MINIATURE

As well as making abstract pictures of pressed flowers, you can also make much more naturalistic designs. For example, the completed miniature illustrated in the photograph on the facing page shows a design that represents as closely as possible the way the plant grows in the wild. I used a small spray of birds-foot trefoil, and although in the finished picture it seems as though it has been pressed just as it was picked, in fact the majority of the piece was dismantled for pressing and reassembled for the picture.

In many cases a natural spray does not seem nearly as attractive when it is presented in two dimensions as it does when seen growing naturally in the wild, when of course it is viewed in three dimensions. For this reason, it is often much more effective to press the different parts of the spray individually and then reconstruct them once they have been pressed. Otherwise, you may find that two leaves cross over and hide a flower or a bud. So, start with a stem and gradually build up your design from that.

There are two ways of approaching the task of finding suitable flowers for miniature work. Either you can sort through your collection looking for all the smallest items, or you can cheat and use parts of larger pieces of pressed flowers or foliage. For instance, a few petals from a large flower can be remade into one that is much smaller.

Another option is to use various parts of a flower in their own right: centres with no petals can make very pretty flowers, and many multi-headed flowers, such as cow parsley, can be dismantled after pressing. If you press it whole, you will have a flower head about 7.5cm (3in) in diameter which can be used as it is, but you also have the option of removing the individual heads to make excellent small flowers and centres. You can even remove individual tiny flowers for use in miniature work.

Try to keep your eyes open when you are looking for flowers to press, as some very unusual items can work extremely well in miniature pictures, such as moss, lichen and tiny pieces of root. Very small buds can be cut in half, which not only makes them flatter but also gives them an added charm in a finished picture.

There are several obvious flowers, such as forget-me-nots, which can either be used as a spray or individually, and wild flowers are often useful as they tend to be small. However, once again I strongly suggest that you grow a collection of wild flowers in your own garden rather than pick them from the countryside and assist in depleting the stocks!

If you are unsure of which flowers will be suitable, or are hard-pressed to think of any small flowers at all, there are many alpine plants that may be ideal. You may also find that browsing through a garden encyclopedia, with coloured illustrations of all the different plants, will fill you with inspiration.

So, if you want to create a successful miniature picture you must think small. Look at plants from all angles to determine how they can be used – maybe you could remove the petals and make a smaller flower with just a few of them?

It takes time, patience and ingenuity to create effective miniature pictures from pressed flowers, making it a fascinating part of the craft for some people. Others will find it far too fiddly and will prefer to continue working on larger, more striking pictures.

Like so many crafts, if you are to enjoy flower pressing to the full you must find the method, materials and styles that suit you best, and you will only do this through trial and error. Do not feel that you have to persist with a particular type of pressed flower work if you are not happy with it. Experiment instead until you find a style in which you want to specialise.

The simplicity of this arrangement of birds-foot trefoil gives it a beauty of its own, and the naturalistic effect is enhanced by the classic frame and mount.

CREATING DIFFERENT EFFECTS

One of the many advantages in working with miniatures is that you can create an enormous variety of different visual effects according to the way in which you group the finished pictures. For example, if you want to hang some miniatures on a large expanse of wall, you will have to use several to create a strong impact – just one picture would be completely lost.

The photograph on the facing page shows various ways in which miniatures can be grouped together to make an effective display. You may find it more pleasing and effective to range together a selection of complementary shapes, rather than just a hotchpotch of squares, circles, ovals and rectangles. For example, on the right-hand side of the photograph, I have placed an oval miniature between two upright rectangles. To give an air of informality, I used different frames and different types of pressed flower design for the two rectangular pictures, making gold the linking theme between the three. However, an equally successful effect would have been achieved using a circular frame between two square ones.

To make the top rectangular picture, I used a card mount in palest pink, behind which I stretched some cream silk. The flowers used were pieces of conifer and some pink heather, with red and white hawthorn flowers to give added colour, plus a little white alyssum. For the central, gold oval design, I used a dusty pink satin backing, on to which I arranged some cow parsley leaves, gypsophila, small 'Marjorie Fair' red roses, some 'Princess' pink potentillas and astrantia. The bottom rectangular picture shows a spray design, made from thalictrum leaves, forget-me-nots and grasses, with 'Marjorie Fair' red roses, hydrangeas and some very small astrantia flowers.

The two pictures hanging on the wooden beam in the left of the photograph perhaps show a more popular way of displaying miniatures, which is nonetheless very attractive. To add a little more interest to the arrangement, I chose gold frames with swivels that resemble the tops of fob watches. The top picture was composed of agrimony leaves and alchemilla flowers, with the addition of a few pink larkspur and red hawthorn flowers. For the bottom picture I used silverweed leaves, plus some pink heather and 'Princess' pink potentilla flowers.

If you have made a sizeable number of miniatures, you could consider displaying them all together, rather than dotting them about your home in collections of ones and twos. For instance, you could create two groups of miniatures in the recesses on either side of a fireplace. Each group can then be arranged within a particular shape, such as a rectangle or square, to give added definition. A charming way of decorating a tiny room, study or minute dining room would be to cover one of the walls with a host of miniatures, so they are almost like wallpaper.

You can use the many different shapes and designs shown in this book for miniature work, as well as larger pictures. In fact, in many cases, the very size of miniatures makes them more suitable for particular ideas and arrangements. For example, if you were thinking of ways of decorating the bedroom of a feminine little girl, you could make a series of miniatures, each bearing a single letter, which when hung together on a wall spelt out her name.

In the same way, you could create a selection of miniatures, as a gift, that all feature the favourite flowers of the recipient. If they were literary-minded, you could even try to include all the flowers mentioned in a particular poem or part of a play – William Shakespeare in particular offers a positive fund of inspiration for ideas of this kind.

Four very different styles of miniature picture are displayed in this photograph, proving that there is plenty of scope for inspiration in even the smallest of designs.

CHAPTER TEN

SENTIMENTAL FLOWERS

Flowers are frequently given as a sign of affection or as an integral part of an important occasion, such as a wedding or anniversary. This chapter shows you how to care for such flowers before they are pressed, and also gives a whole range of ideas for sentimental flower pictures.

Preparing the Flowers

Ideally, one should be aware in advance that the flowers used for a special occasion are going to be pressed, as there are several points to bear in mind.

First, the flowers themselves should be suitable for pressing – there is no point in offering to press someone's wedding flowers when their bouquet consists of, say, chrysanthemums, pale carnations, large daisies or gerberas, since none of these flowers press successfully at all. The result will be disappointing, not only for you but also for the bride who has been looking forward to keeping her flowers for ever. So, you must either plan the flowers that are to be pressed in advance, or check that the flowers already used are suitable.

Second, if one does know in advance that the celebratory flowers are to be pressed, there are various details that can be given to the florist in question that will make one's task much easier. As little wiring as possible should be used, because every time a wire is pushed through a rose petal, for example, it leaves two small marks that remain even when the petal has been pressed. It is also usual practice to spray a bouquet with water from an atomiser to keep it fresh, but it should be avoided in this case as the water droplets can mark the flowers, as well as possibly make the bouquet damp when the time comes for you to press it.

Timing is also of the essence – flowers can be sent to you through the post as soon as the special event is over, but the best option is to be able to press them on the very day that they are used. Perhaps the only occasion suggested in this chapter where you wouldn't want to press the flowers immediately is on Valentine's Day. Even so, being tempted into keeping the flowers until they are past their best will mean that you won't have a satisfactory pressed flower picture with which to remember them. Instead, you have to take a long-term view, realising that although you cannot enjoy them as fresh flowers for very long, you will be able to admire a beautiful picture for many years to come.

Having planned in advance that you intend to press a bouquet or some special flowers, you must also decide how you intend to transport them from the event to your home. If you just place them on the back seat of your car, or they are removed from an arrangement and not packed up in any special way, some of the petals will almost definitely become bruised, which will cause brown lines, patches and spots once the flowers have been pressed. Using a wedding bouquet as an example, and assuming that you are either attending the function or collecting the bouquet afterwards, you should make up a simple box, such as the one shown in the photograph. It should have a hole at one end, in which the handle of the bouquet can rest to keep the flowers away from the sides of the box. You should also make a bed on which the flowers can lie from plenty of clean but crumpled tissue paper, also gently tucking it around the sides of the bouquet for added protection.

There may be occasions when the time involved in the journey home means that you would arrive with a pile of wilted, or even dead, flowers, in which case there must be some forward planning. If you ensure that you have packed the suitable equipment in a suitcase or the boot of your car, you should be able to solve all these problems. If the plant material needs to go in a press, a small one is probably adequate for your needs, and will not be too heavy to carry, and if it should be pressed between the pages of books, then take a supply of blotting paper and telephone directories with you.

Many of these ideas using sentimental flowers take some extra thought and planning, but the end result, and the enthusiasm with which they will be received, is well worth the effort.

When pressing flowers from an arrangement, only choose the best specimens and carefully pack them in a box if taking them home.

PRESSING A
WEDDING BOUQUET

For any bride who wants a permanent memento of her wedding, a pressed picture of her bouquet is perhaps the most unusual and attractive reminder of all. It is almost impossible to recreate a wedding bouquet completely accurately, as the original bouquet is three-dimensional and not flat like the picture. Nevertheless, you can look at the shape of the bouquet and reproduce it in the finished design. In this case, the bouquet was a curved shower, the shape of which I tried to recreate in the picture shown opposite.

There is a wealth of beautiful fabrics that you can use as backgrounds to pressed bouquets, ranging from wonderful silks to antique pieces of lace. The material that I used was a lovely heavy cream bridal fabric, chosen because it was the closest equivalent I could find to the bride's dress – surprisingly enough, she wouldn't let me chop a hole in the real thing! If the dress is being specially made for the bride it should be an easy matter to ask for an extra piece of the fabric with which to create the background, but since this is often not the case, a compromise must be reached. Apart from bridal fabrics and laces, you can also use one of the beautiful and unusual papers that resemble lace or have a shimmery self-pattern.

It is extremely important that you press more pieces from the bouquet than you think you will need, as some of the plant material may turn brown in the press or emerge pressed into the wrong shape. You will then still have enough material with which to create an attractive picture, rather than try to make a suitable design from a few odds and ends.

The original bouquet for this picture was exceptionally large, so I have not been able to reproduce a life-sized replica but instead have scaled it down to fit into a picture frame. You may find that you often have to do this, as even a modest wedding bouquet can be too large to fit into a reasonably-sized picture frame, and if it were reproduced in its original size it could become such a large picture that it would completely dominate any room in which it was hung. So, a little artistic licence may be called for, and you will have to use your skills to create a bouquet picture that gives the feeling of the wedding flowers without reproducing them exactly.

Having pressed all the component parts to make up a wedding picture for the bride, there may be some pieces left over (if you have followed my advice and pressed additional flowers and foliage in case of accident). You could use these to make up some smaller pictures for the bridesmaids, or perhaps the mothers of the newly married couple. For the bridesmaids, you could use fabric from their dresses as the background, or if that is not possible, choose a cream silk backing with a mount in the same colour as their outfits.

If, for example, the bridesmaids all wore deep pink dresses, you could use a gold oval frame with the appropriate fabric as backing, assuming that you have access to some matching material. If that is not possible, you could perhaps use a deep pink card mount with a cream silk backing, and a narrow gold frame. In the case of the bridesmaids and mothers, it might be better just to make little posy-style arrangements, or any other design that you especially enjoy creating, rather than a particular bridal bouquet shape.

To make the picture of the bridal bouquet shown in the photograph on the facing page, I used rose leaves and some asparagus fern for the foliage, which I then softened with pieces of pink heather and small sprays of gypsophila. The flowers themselves were pink roses, cream roses, some cream spray, pink-edged, carnations, some white larkspur and white stephanotis.

Making a pressed flower picture from a wedding bouquet provides a lasting, and beautiful, reminder of a very memorable and special day. It may be impossible to recreate the bouquet exactly, but you should still be able to reproduce the shape.

FIRST VALENTINE ROSES

Nothing can be more exciting than the first time that you are given some flowers, and particularly red roses. They have a very special significance, and how I wish I had known how to press flowers when I was given my first red roses by my husband, but unfortunately I learnt a few years too late! However, I do still have a squashed, rather brown and mildewy rose pressed between the pages of a book somewhere, so I suppose that could be classed as my first attempt!

As I mentioned in the chapter describing the actual techniques of pressing (*see pp. 36–45*), it is essential to dismantle red roses, or any roses of the hybrid tea or floribunda varieties, and to press them as individual petals. You must also remember to press some of the other parts of the roses, such as the sepals and perhaps even the centres, as these will prove to be useful later on when you come to reassemble them into a design.

Once the red roses have been pressed, you can consider what type of design you want to create. In the picture shown in the photograph on the facing page, I chose a walnut oval frame with a gold line around the edge, and used a plain cream silk as the background, as I felt that this showed the roses to their best advantage.

This is not the easiest selection of flowers to use in a design as they all look the same, and apart from turning some of the rose petals into buds, it is hard to introduce any interesting variations into the shapes in the picture. As the real stems were discarded because they were too bulky, I used the stems of the rose leaves and the gypsophila instead. To make the roses I arranged five petals in an overlapping circle, placed three petals on top of them and then finally positioned the rose centre in the middle. If you are using a lot of roses in your pressed flower pictures, you may find it worthwhile making up a small stock of finished roses in different colours to save time when you are in an inspired mood and want to concentrate on a design rather than the various techniques involved.

The rose buds were made by arranging three petals in a bud shape, one on top of the other but with their edges showing, and then placing three sepals over the top of the bud to give a realistic touch of green.

I began the basic structure of the rose leaves in the bottom left of the picture and then built up the shape with the larger open roses, tucking the asparagus fern and gypsophila behind them, and finally put the buds into position. However, there is no formal way to create this design, and the way you approach it will be determined by the number of roses you have to press and the shape of the leaves in the rest of the bouquet. Once I had created the spray shape that I wanted, I tied the red ribbon that had accompanied the bouquet into a small flat bow, to minimise its lumpiness, and added it to the design.

It can be very rewarding pressing flowers that have a sentimental significance, whether the finished picture is intended for you or someone else. The flowers give double pleasure, both from their particular meaning to the recipient and also from their beauty as a pressed flower picture. It is always much more difficult to produce a lovely picture that contains only one type of flower, such as a bunch of freesias, as you can only use one flower shape, although you will be able to press the flowers in various ways – for example, side views, full views, with buds and without. However, if you have a mixed bouquet, there may be both small and large flowers that can be used, as well as different shapes to add interest to the picture.

When thinking about this design, I decided that it would be a charming idea to incorporate all the elements that accompanied the bouquet of roses. This included the ribbon that decorated the bouquet, which I have actually placed in the picture itself, with the card and some of the pretty wrapping paper taped to the back of the frame.

EIGHTEENTH BIRTHDAY PICTURE

The benefits of planning in advance the flowers for a special occasion are fully demonstrated in the photograph on the facing page. Having talked to the person making the eighteenth birthday cake about our individual requirements, we chose some suitable flowers to fit a small silver vase that was placed on top of the cake, and once the guests had gone I hurried them into the presses I had taken with me to the party.

Of course, it is not necessary to press the actual flowers from the birthday celebration itself, as one could just make a picture for the eighteen-year old as a present. Most girls would love a flower picture for their bedrooms, and if it has a sentimental significance as well then it will be even more appreciated.

In this case, the flowers had to be fairly small to fit the cake vase, so the finished picture itself was equally small. Using a profusion of small flowers in a large frame only makes a muddled, confused mess so one must always bear in mind the scale of the pressed material available for the picture. Here, I used an outline of rose leaves and asparagus fern interspersed with London Pride, and used 'Princess' pink potentillas, the patio rose 'Gentle Touch' and some stephanotis.

It is always wise to first check with the recipient the colour scheme of the room in which the picture will be displayed, as it is possible to vary the emphasis placed upon the colours within the picture accordingly. For example, this selection of flowers could have been framed in a pale green mount, or the entire design could have been created on a very pale blue-grey background with no mount at all, both of which would have given a very different emphasis to the pink roses. In this case a gold frame was chosen to match another picture in the bedroom, but it would also have looked attractive in a pastel pink frame or one made from pine or a darker wood, depending on the room for which it was intended.

Bedrooms are very popular display areas for pressed flower pictures, perhaps because they are gentle and attractive wall decorations that can blend well with the soft tones many people like to use in their bedrooms. I once made a very pretty montage of framed pictures for a friend to go over the bed which, when assembled, made a rectangle as wide as the bed and about 60cm (2ft) high. The set of pictures was planned by arranging the empty frames on the floor, and I placed two long narrow designs (*see pp. 76–7*) at each end, with the smaller ones making a symmetrical pattern in the middle. In all, to make the collection 1.6m (5ft) wide, there were about ten pictures, and the finished effect was absolutely stunning. All the pictures had matching frames and a pinky-peach colour scheme, but every picture was an individual design and completely different from its fellow.

Another very successful collection of my pictures has been made by a lady who is very keen on yellow roses. She has now collected about nine or ten of my pictures, all of which contain some yellow roses, and has grouped them together beautifully in a small alcove. They include a small circular picture with a bronze fabric backing and a small spray of miniature yellow roses, plus several ovals with cream and gold backgrounds. There is also a fairly large picture with a dark brown mount around which has been drawn three gold lines, enclosing a spray design, and a small square picture with a brown handmade paper as a backing, which is one of my favourites. The others are mainly rectangular with cream surrounds and gold material backings. The blending of all the colours, with the theme of yellow roses running throughout the collection, is extremely effective, and I might even start collecting something like that myself!

Such a pretty yet elegant pressed flower picture as this one would make an ideal gift for a girl's eighteenth birthday, especially if it matches the decor of her bedroom.

SILVER WEDDING FLOWERS

This picture could either be made for yourself or as a gift for someone else, and I think it is a lovely way of celebrating such a special occasion as a silver wedding anniversary.

I was able to make the background from part of the original wedding dress, which was unlikely to be worn again by the erstwhile bride. (As twenty-five years had elapsed, she didn't mind me cutting it up!) So a choice of background was easy, but if you do not have access to a piece of the relevant dress you can either cheat and buy a similar fabric, or choose a plain white silk or satin backing.

For a silver wedding picture, it seemed appropriate to use a silver theme, so the oval frame shown in the facing photograph was an obvious but perfect choice. However, you could easily choose a different style of silver frame, or even a greyish frame instead.

The flowers were mainly chosen to accentuate the overall silvery effect, but some of them also came from the 'bride's' garden, as I felt this would give the picture additional meaning for her. The basic shape was composed of silverweed leaves, with some sea lavender tucked in between them, then the largest blue delphiniums were positioned around the curve. I then added the pink and cream roses, as well as some wild and some cultivated patio roses. Next, to fill out the curve, I used the lovely *Alchemilla alpina* leaves since they have such a perfect silver finish. Finally, I added some *Astrantia minor* and iberis flowers.

The idea of making a special flower picture to commemorate a particular wedding anniversary works very well. Another successful choice would be a golden wedding anniversary.

In this case, you could make the whole picture golden, choosing a gold frame, making the backing from a piece of gold velvet or silk, and then using gold-coloured leaves and flowers for the design itself. However, you may find it more successful to introduce more contrasting colour elements into your design. Using the gold frame and choosing either a rectangular or oval shape, you could then use a mid-brown mount with a gold line drawn around the aperture, and choose a plain cream or light beige silk or satin backing with a combination of flowers in various autumnal shades with some darker brown or green leaves, to help show off the flowers to their best advantage. The number of flowers that can be used for the golden theme is quite large: you could choose something very simple, such as a small spray of yellow roses with a few of their own leaves and buds, or something more complicated, such as a mixture of yellow roses, mimosa, potentillas and narcissi, with a few primroses and primulas to give extra detail.

There are several other wedding anniversaries that would make successful flower pictures – for instance, for the bronze anniversary it would be very interesting to find a coppery frame and some flowers to match. Another idea would be the lace anniversary, when you could perhaps arrange some cow parsley over a fabric lace background. For the china anniversary you could create a small picture in a porcelain frame.

There are also some unusual slants on the wedding anniversary themes. For example, to commemorate a wood anniversary, as well as using a wooden frame, you could make a collage with pressed pieces of bark from a variety of trees. For the pearl anniversary, you could create a picture in shades of cream and grey and, using the tiniest seed pearls you can find, add them as small sprays almost like sweet pea tendrils. It's amazing the ideas that can come to mind with a little thought and some extra effort on your part.

To make this silver anniversary picture, you could either press the flowers used to celebrate the day itself or you could press a selection of flowers beforehand and give the finished picture as a present at the time of the anniversary.

Ruby Wedding Picture

If you have always found it very difficult to dream up original and unusual ideas for ruby weddings, then making a red or burgundy pressed flower picture could solve all your problems.

There are many choices of frame that might fit in with this theme. For example, there are some very attractive red lacquered frames which could be very useful, you could choose a dark mahogany frame with a reddish tinge, or even a gold or wood frame if it sets off a dark red mount or background. In the case of the picture shown opposite, I found a beautiful frame, with a lovely wide gold band on the inner side of the frame that is decorated with red and green flowers and leaves.

There are several backings you could choose, from some maroon, burgundy or ruby papers to many different mount cards. Alternatively you could use a dark red velvet or watered silk, but I chose a very dark cream silk to counteract the busy effect of the frame. The dark cream also sets off the bright red roses well – had I chosen a white satin, card or fabric in a similar shade it would have been too bright and could have detracted from the frame.

The shape of this design could best be described as a spray, the two outer points being provided by pieces of vetch, and the other leaves being rose and Japanese maple. The latter has lovely tones but is not always an easy leaf to use as its heavy colouring can make it difficult to incorporate into a design. I then tucked some heuchera flowers between the foliage. The flowers were built up next, starting with the biggest, which were the bright red roses 'Eyepaint' and 'Robin Redbreast'. The design was then filled out with the smaller red roses, 'Yesterday' and 'Marjorie Fair', and finally to complete any gaps I used some pink 'Ballerina' and creamy pink 'Penelope' roses.

If you have chosen a rich red silk or card background then it may be better to use flowers in tones of cream and gold, as dark backings work best with light flowers.

However, there are many red flowers that could make a successful choice.

For example, if the recipients of the picture love fuchsias, you could create a large spray of fuchsias with their own leaves. This is a very popular design, but unfortunately many varieties of fuchsia do not press well, turning brown and fading even before they have been removed from the press. The smaller varieties are usually the most successful, and I would particularly recommend the small outdoor varieties, as they seem to take better to pressing than the larger and lumpier types.

Other possible red flowers include geums. They can be temperamental in the press, but look really lovely when pressed successfully. There are also red potentillas and red hawthorn, to name but two, and you will find many more on looking through this book.

I think that wedding anniversaries make very suitable subjects for pressed flower pictures, and there can't be many that don't lend themselves to a suitable picture. For example, for a diamond anniversary you could create a diamond-shaped picture, so try a little lateral thinking if at first an idea doesn't come to mind.

Wedding anniversaries			
1	Paper	15	Crystal
2	Cotton	20	China
3	Leather	25	Silver
4	Fruit and flowers	30	Pearl
5	Wood	35	Coral
6	Sugar	40	Ruby
7	Wool	50	Golden
8	Bronze	55	Emerald
9	Pottery	60	Diamond
10	Tin	65	Sapphire
12	Silk and fine linen	70	Platinum

The beautifully rich tones of this picture lend themselves well to a ruby wedding anniversary.

WELCOME TO YOUR NEW HOME PICTURE

This idea first emerged when a friend was moving house upon her retirement. She was going to a flat which would have very little growing space, apart from the odd window box, and was leaving behind an extremely beautiful garden that contained many years of memories. It therefore seemed logical to press a little of every suitable plant in her garden and later to create a design from it that would remind her for many years to come of her treasured garden.

Although many people do not make such a dramatic move from a very special garden to a flat, most of us leave a few favourite plants behind when we move house, so framing a few of them serves as a lovely reminder of times gone by. It is also a very effective, yet thoroughly personal, way of welcoming someone into their new home.

The design shown in the photograph on the facing page uses a number of different elements. A curve is a good shape to choose if there are plenty of items that you wish to include in the picture, as it can accommodate quite a lot of material. For the foliage in the picture, I used some silverweed, *Alchemilla alpina*, some grey 'curry plant', sea lavender, a little pink heather and a few grey bramble leaves. The flowers are some large *Hellebore atrorubens* and some light blue delphiniums. For the background, I chose a pale cream silk and a mount of pale blue-grey, with a plain gold frame to make the picture fit as well as possible into a colour scheme as yet unknown.

Not knowing the decorative style of the new home is an important point to bear in mind when planning a picture of this sort, so it is always best to choose colours and frames that are attractive without being so dramatic or colourful that you considerably reduce their hanging potential. Of course, you will have more scope if you know that the recipient will decorate each room in a particular shade, because they never do anything else!

Obviously this idea has to be thought out in advance, and if your friend or family move during the winter then you could be faced with a big problem in trying to gather enough material to make an attractive and interesting picture. Perhaps this is the perfect excuse to be allowed to pick a selection of all the suitable plants from the gardens of all your friends and family, just in case! You will then have the right specimens ready and waiting whenever anyone decides to up sticks and move.

If friends are foolhardy but kind enough to let you loose in their gardens, it is a very nice idea to make them a small picture from some of the flowers you have gathered and subsequently pressed. Even if they are not moving, it is still a charming way of saying 'thank you'. The only potential problem with friends being eager to let you pick bits and pieces from their gardens is that often they may not grow anything that is suitable for pressing. Unfortunately, many people seem to take it as a personal insult (on behalf of their garden) if one says that there aren't really any plants or flowers worth pressing, so to prevent any hurt feelings I usually try to pick a few items that are possible candidates for pressing, which seems to go down much better than completely refusing someone's kind offer.

Using sentimental flowers in a picture as a present is a sure-fire recipe for success. Whether it is something as special as a wedding bouquet or as simple as a few flowers gathered on a picnic outing together, knowing where and when the flowers were picked or used adds a great deal to the meaning of the picture, and the recipient will be very touched at your thoughtful and generous gesture. As an extra reminder, you could write a special message on a pretty piece of card and fix it to the back of the picture, noting both the date and the event.

Making a pressed flower picture as a way of welcoming someone into their new home is both a charming and original idea, especially if it uses flowers from their previous garden.

Holiday Flowers

My holiday in Portugal last year found me ready and equipped. I had packed a small pair of sharp folding scissors and a supply of blotting paper. If one runs out of the latter one can use paper tissues instead, though I wouldn't recommend them for pressing fragile flower heads as the tissues can leave a slight pattern on the petals. However, they are ideal for leaves and stems.

I had a rough idea in my mind, before going to Portugal, of the approximate shape and design of the picture I wanted to create. The arched terracotta mount was chosen to remind me of the colour and style of Portuguese houses, and the frame was another easy choice because we saw so much dark wood furniture there. The foliage was gathered in the mountains of the Algarve and consists of stems of eucalyptus and sage, the scent of which was very strong in that area, and it mingled deliciously with that of the pine trees just above us. The flowers, including some yellow potentillas, were picked from the garden of the villa in which we stayed.

It is obviously every bit as important to respect the wild flowers in a foreign country as it is in one's own, and not to pick large quantities of anything as you will only need a few pieces to create a floral souvenir of your trip. If you are visiting a city and there are no suitable plants around, then why not buy some local flowers from a florist or market? If you press even one or two types of flower you could possibly decorate a photograph of your holiday with a pressed flower mount (*see pp. 136–7*).

I felt that the design for this holiday picture should be a natural and less structured design than normal, so I laid out the pressed stems of eucalyptus which naturally fell into a fan shape and used that as the basis of my design.

Many other themes came to mind when I started thinking about holiday pictures. For example, you could use some locally made fabric as a background, or if you spent a lot of time of the beach, you could press some seaweed and later incorporate it into the picture. Seaweed presses beautifully, but needs a slightly different technique, so take it back to your hotel or villa and deal with it in the bathroom! Fill the wash basin with lukewarm water and rinse the seaweed repeatedly. Once you think it is clean, rinse it again a couple of times to make absolutely sure, fill the basin with cold water and place one strand of seaweed in the basin at a time. Then, taking a large sheet of blotting paper, sink it into the water and bring it up, flat, beneath the seaweed. Spread out the seaweed into the shape in which it is to be pressed while still in the water, then slowly lift it out of the basin, keeping it flat, let it drip for a while and then place it on a waterproof surface. Continue in this way until all the seaweed has been prepared, then cover each piece with a clean sheet of blotting paper and place a couple of newspapers over the top. Pile up all the layers of seaweed in the same way as you would ordinary pressed material (*see p. 38*) and leave them overnight, lightly weighted down with a couple of books. You will have to change and dry the blotting paper frequently during the next few days, so either take a good stock with you, or carefully remove one sheet at a time and iron it dry before replacing it. The seaweed should then be left for a month.

One way of using the seaweed would be to use some very fine towelling as the background to give a beachy feel to the picture, and incorporate some minute shells, as the material would absorb their shape, thus allowing the glass to lie flat against the plant material.

Depending on how exciting your holiday was, you could make some really exotic pictures, perhaps using some tiny shells, seaweed, brightly coloured tropical flowers and some pearls. The ideas are limitless and it is up to you to spare a few moments when on holiday to notice what is growing around you and press some interesting pieces that you will be able to use on your return.

NINETIETH BIRTHDAY CELEBRATIONS

This picture can either be given as a present for a ninetieth birthday, or made from some flowers that were presented on the day itself. It is such a landmark that it seems a shame to let it pass without making a permanent reminder of this important occasion. After all, flowers always make very successful presents, but long-lasting ones, such as pressed flower pictures, are doubly appreciated.

Any birthday celebrations always seem to be over as swiftly as they begin, and the anticipation is probably just as important as the event itself, but a pressed flower picture can serve as a lovely memento.

You will usually find that there is a favourite flower that you can use, or perhaps a particular colour, for a picture such as this. For example, if the recipient loves freesias, you can either press some bright yellow freesias and create a picture of autumnal shades, or press some mauve and cream freesias and incorporate them in a picture with blue or pink colouring.

The other possibility for this particular birthday was to press some flowers used at the birthday party or some of the flowers received as gifts. If you are giving the fresh flowers yourself, you have the ideal opportunity of holding a few back and pressing them immediately. You can then make the picture at your leisure, knowing that the flowers were pressed in peak condition. It is far easier to buy some extra flowers or to pick an additional bunch from your garden, than to explain to someone that you would like to take some of your gift home with you in order to give it back to them again at a later date!

Special cards are always appreciated at times like these – my grandmother says that cards are her favourite part of the proceedings. A pressed flower card can not only be enjoyed with the others but can then be framed and hung as a picture (*see pp. 130–1*).

Another successful birthday picture was as an accompaniment to a pair of 'Ballerina' and 'Marjorie Fair' rose bushes. I made a picture from the same flowers to show what the rose bushes would yield the following summer. Another avenue to explore is the possibility of pressing the flower belonging to the month of the birthday in question. In some cases the particular flower may not press well, but if, for example, the stone and flower were sapphire and lily of the valley, you could create a beautiful combination, perhaps with a sapphire-coloured background with a paler blue mount and a silver frame, and then a simple arrangement of lilies of the valley which would stand out very well against the blue backing.

You can also investigate the language of flowers. There are several versions, so you can always bend them slightly! You could make a very simple picture with pansies, which are generally translated as 'think of me', or potentillas which mean 'beloved daughter'. Alternatively you can use the actual name of the flower, such as forget-me-not. If you intend to use the language of flowers to send a message on your card or picture it might be a good idea to put a rough translation on the back or inside the card to avoid confusion, just in case there is more than one meaning for a particular flower!

Finally, if you have a friend with a floral name you could create a picture around the flower they have been named after. For instance, you could make a herbal picture for someone called Rosemary, or a lovely wintry picture with holly, hellebores and carnations for a Holly. Thinking of different pressed flower ideas for birthday presents should keep you going for a while!

For this picture, I chose some of the flowers that the recipient can see from her window. Arranging them in a curved shape, I used a small fern, some gorse, a few 'Canary Bird' roses and some pansies. I found a piece of blue-grey silk for the background, to tone in with the recipient's decor, and selected the wooden frame and the gold tones in the picture itself for the same reason.

CHAPTER ELEVEN

DESIGNING WITH PRESSED FLOWERS

This chapter will inspire you to design other items and incorporate pressed flowers in other crafts. Pressed flowers can be used as a basic shape in stencil designs, or used to create a tapestry or needlework design.

CREATING A TAPESTRY

Pressed flowers have many more uses than one might at first imagine, and as well as being used in their own right, they can also serve as the inspiration for further designs.

For example, the photograph on the previous page shows how pressed flower designs can be used to decorate photograph frames. Here, a British chain store reproduced my original designs in what turned out to be a very successful venture. With a little work and care (*see pp. 136–7*), you can achieve a similar effect.

Pressed flowers can be used on many other printed objects, and not necessarily for commercial purposes. You could use them as a decorative device on invitations, or as part of the design on your personal writing paper. Despite worries to the contrary, pressed flowers photograph well and make a refreshing change from more conventional forms of artwork.

For many people, their love of flowers extends to many other crafts besides that of flower arranging, and especially needlework and tapestry. The photograph opposite shows a tapestry design that has been reproduced from the pressed flower picture that stands beside it. Although this tapestry was commissioned by a commercial company, it is an idea that could easily be tried at home.

First decide what item you wish to make. For instance, you could choose a cushion, chair seat or bell pull, though you may wish to make something relatively simple and uncomplicated on your first attempt. Once you have determined its size and shape, cut out a piece of card that is a few centimetres (inches) bigger all round. Arrange your pressed flower design on the piece of card, trying to keep the colours as harmonious as possible. Once you are happy with the overall design, fix it in position with rubber solution adhesive as firmly as possible. You can use more glue than normal as the picture will not be displayed, and it is essential that the flowers should remain in their exact position.

You should then trace the design on to a sheet of tracing paper, either tracing directly from the flowers or first covering them with a sheet of glass before beginning your tracing. You will find it helpful to work in a good light.

Once you have drawn all the outlines of the basic design on to the tracing paper, you can then transfer them to the canvas or linen that you are using. Draw in a pale outline at first, then strengthen it with a strong ink or pencil, which will give a better guideline. Since you will be constantly referring to your picture for colour reference I would recommend keeping it under glass and just taping the sides very firmly to stop the flowers being damaged.

This may seem to be a difficult way of creating a tapestry or some embroidery, but if you are skilled at needlework you will find it extremely satisfying to have made something from your own design.

To create the design shown in the photograph, I used a selection of autumn leaves, brambles, Virginia creeper and some alchemilla. The flowers include roses, potentillas and hellebores, and the shape is another example of the wreath design (*see pp. 78–9*). The warm, somewhat muted, colours lend themselves very well to a tapestry design.

Although this is a very complicated example of pressed flower design, you could try some far more simple ideas. For example, you could create the design for a simple piece of embroidery using small sprays of pressed flowers, or make an initial design from pressed flowers that could be transferred on to squared paper and used to embroider a handkerchief. Both of these ideas would make marvellous presents, and you could perhaps place the finished embroidery in a tissue-lined box that has been decorated with pressed flowers or ribbons.

Once you begin, you will find plenty of inspiration for creating tapestries and embroideries from pressed flower designs.

MAKING STENCILS

Pressed flower shapes can easily lend themselves to stencil designs, as they are already two-dimensional, and are therefore easy to trace. There is also a limitless number of shapes that can be made from pressed material, so you need never run out of inspiration.

In the photograph on the facing page, there is a design made up from four wild roses and four sprays of wild rose leaves, with four individual rose leaves arranged at angles between them. When creating a stencil design, it is essential to remember to leave a space between each leaf or flower shape, otherwise the stencil card will drop to pieces when it is cut out. This is because the stencil is the reverse image of the design itself, so each detail must be shown clearly.

Once you have chosen a suitable design, place it on a sheet of firm card and carefully arrange it in position, bearing in mind the scale of your required pattern. There is no need to worry too much about the colour of the flowers and foliage that you will be using, as you can change those when you use the stencil. Just because you want a pale, peach-coloured border for a room doesn't mean that you are restricted to using similar-coloured flowers when planning the design: you could even create the design using brown leaves and blue flowers, providing their shapes are satisfactory.

So, once you are happy with the shapes and their positions, you can glue the plant material in place. Again, you should fix the pieces very firmly to their card backing with a rubber solution adhesive, to stop them moving about or even falling off. Then, place a sheet of glass over the design and trace the outlines on to the stiff card that you will be using for your stencil pattern. Once the design has been traced, you must then cut it out very carefully with a very sharp knife. To do this, place the stencil card on top of a hard, even surface, such as a sheet of hardboard or a special designer's cutting board. Otherwise you may completely ruin your kitchen table or working surface! Make two or three tracings of the design to enable you to experiment with various groupings and arrangements, and also to allow for any mistakes you make in cutting, especially on your first attempt. Try to make the cut outlines as clean as possible, since any mistakes or wobbly lines will be reproduced every time you use the stencil.

Apart from the ideas shown in this chapter, there are several other ways of incorporating pressed flowers into hobbies. Porcelain painting is just one possibility, and if you create a suitable pressed flower design it can then be copied on to a piece of china, which makes a change from using fresh flowers as the reference material.

Another hobby of mine in which I have used pressed flowers as a design tool is in cake decorating. Having iced the cake with a plain layer of royal icing and then left it to dry, I have made copies of small pressed flower pictures both on the top, as a centrepiece, and with small sprays around the sides of the cake.

Having first transferred the shapes on to a piece of tracing paper, I find it easiest to almost trace the designs on to the cake, piercing through the outlines into the icing at regular intervals with a special cake scriber, or a sharp pin. This creates the basic outlines and from there I work by eye with a small piping nozzle and several different colours of royal icing. This idea may not be suitable for a real beginner, but if anyone is really enthusiastic about cake decorating it should not take long to acquire the necessary skills, enabling them to create some lovely and different effects.

There are several books available that are full of ideas and information on using stencils, whether on walls or to decorate pieces of furniture. You can use either an emulsion paint or an oil-based paint with the stencil, although if you make any mistakes with the emulsion it should be easy to wash it off and start again.

CHAPTER TWELVE

PRESSED FLOWERS AS PRESENTS

Once you have mastered the art of both pressing and presenting flowers in a professional manner, there are many gifts that you can create. Included in this chapter are stationery items, a pressed flower mirror, a decorated photograph mount and several other ideas that will inspire you to experiment with your skills.

GREETINGS CARDS AND GIFT TAGS

Pressed flowers make marvellous decorations for stationery products, and there are a great many ways in which they can be used. The cost need not be very high and you will have the satisfaction of knowing that the finished result will be kept for a long time, if not forever, by the recipient.

The general technique used for stationery decoration is to cover the flowers with a clear adhesive film, which not only protects them from damp or dirt, but also holds them in position.

The film is available from larger stationers and art suppliers, and it is also used to protect the covers of books. There is usually a square grid of lines on the backing, which makes it easy to cut it in straight lines, and a small roll can cover quite a few items. Alternatively, many picture framers have some heat-sealing equipment, and are prepared to seal items for you.

If you choose this method, do take an enormous amount of care when transporting the items to the framer, to prevent them being damaged. I would suggest that you glue the flowers in position to prevent problems, or carry them sandwiched between two sheets of glass. However, once you hand over your work to the framer, you cannot always guarantee that the design will not have moved slightly, so on the whole it is probably best to use a cold-seal film at home, unless the item is extremely important and you want to achieve as professional a finish as possible.

First decide whether you wish to make a portrait or landscape design, and check that the card will stand up properly if you are opting for the latter shape. Any flowers can be used, but take care to get the scale exactly right – using just one very large flower can look rather out of place, and if the flowers you wish to use are tiny, it will need a very complicated design to fill the card.

Various suggestions are shown in the facing photograph. In a clockwise direction from the top left of the picture, the card next to the clock was decorated with some bramble leaves, grass and wild roses. Immediately next to it is a design made from Japanese maple flowers, Russian ivy flowers, astrantia and some pink larkspur. The card below it shows three 'Marjorie Fair' roses, a few alchemilla flowers and the leaves and tendrils of some old man's beard. I drew a fine border around all three gift tags to emphasise the design, and they contain a selection of flowers: a fuchsia with one of its own leaves; the leaves of some old man's beard and some cotton flowers; some phlox and its leaves.

The photograph on page 129 shows a group of parcels, arranged under a Christmas tree, that have been decorated with pressed flowers. You should use a plain paper, to give a good background for the pressed flowers, and ensure that it is fairly thick to absorb the glue without becoming transparent.

First wrap your parcels securely in the chosen paper, ensuring that all the folds and flaps are as neat as possible. You should then decide which area of parcel is going to be decorated with the pressed flowers and foliage. Tie some pretty ribbon around the parcel, ensuring that you leave the chosen area free. Whenever possible you should try to co-ordinate the colour of the ribbon with that of the flowers, otherwise the effect may not be as successful as you would have wished.

Working on a clean, flat surface, decide exactly where you wish to place the flowers, and then arrange them on a horizontal level first so that they do not slip off. Glue them in position with some rubber solution adhesive, ensuring that they are firmly fixed to the paper without the glue being visible. You can then turn the parcel round if you wish to decorate more than one of its faces.

These cards have been protected with a heat-sealing machine, but you can produce excellent results with a cold-seal film.

PRESSED FLOWER BOOKMARKS AND OTHER IDEAS

Another idea for a small gift is to decorate a bookmark. Pressed flowers are at their best when kept inside books, and retain their colour for many years. I have seen Victorian bookmarks where the colours are still beautiful some ninety years later!

In the case of the bookmarks shown in the photograph on the opposite page, I drew a border around the section that encloses the flowers, not only to give them additional definition but also because the parallel lines at the base help to decorate the bookmark. However, you could just use a perfectly plain piece of card or, alternatively, one that has some calligraphy incorporated into the design, some pretty scroll work, or anything else that appeals to you, and then seal it.

The bookmarks shown here were decorated with a mixture of flowers and foliage. Working clockwise from the top left hand corner, is a bookmark decorated with two 'Marjorie Fair' roses and some asparagus fern; a bookmark decorated with bramble leaves, alchemilla flowers and three 'Yesterday' roses; one using verbena flowers, male hop flowers and old man's beard; and a bookmark using two wild roses and their leaves, with some small pieces of Russian vine.

Pressed flowers can be used to decorate many other stationery ideas besides the ones shown here. For example, a pressed flower design can make a lovely picture for a calendar, or you could create an appropriate design for each month of the year, composed of seasonal flowers.

You can also use the cold-seal film (*see pp. 130–1*) to cover the fronts of notebooks, diaries, address books and photograph albums once they have been decorated with a pressed flower design. Another suggestion is to decorate trays, mats and coasters, although you will get better results taking them to a framer to be professionally heat-sealed, so they will better withstand the heat from a plate or teapot.

Bookmarks that also carry a message can be very popular, giving you an opportunity to research the enormous and fascinating language of flowers. Pansies are a very popular flower and have different meanings according to their colour. For instance, the yellow pansy can mean 'souvenirs', or 'the oceans may part us but my heart is still with you' and the purple pansy means 'memories of time with you'.

There are many other flowers which press well and bear charming meanings, some of which are listed below. I should add that there are also a great many flowers that seem to have rather negative meanings, such as the lovely little lawn daisy, which apparently means 'delay', or 'return after a few days when I may give you an answer' – not necessarily the most suitable text to put on a bookmark.

Here are several other suggestions that would make excellent messages for various occasions, and provide a very different way of expressing your feelings:

Ivy leaves – tenacity; my love for you is strong

Jasmine – elegance; I admire your taste

Oak leaves – courage; take heart

Pink phlox – friendship

White phlox – I would like to get to know you better

Broom – devotion; I am yours for ever

Cineraria – delight; I enjoy your company

Honeysuckle – true love

Agrimony – gratitude; please accept my thanks

Rosemary – your memory will never fade

White hyacinth – admiration

Whatever flower you choose, it is a good idea to write the meaning next to it, in case there is more than one and your good intentions lead to a misunderstanding!

DECORATED SHEET MUSIC

Many of us have a special tune or song that conjures up a particular time and place whenever we hear it, or brings back a flood of memories, but we may have no way of celebrating it. However, making a decorated and framed picture of the sheet music is a marvellous way of doing just that, and has the added benefit of being a very unusual and original idea for a present.

There are several ways of approaching the decoration of music. One could choose a song title with a special sentimental attachment, or the frontispiece from the score of some classical music (as shown in the photograph on the facing page), but there are other ideas too from which you can choose.

If the song is a modern piece, the front sheet may well be a photograph or picture, in which case one could pick a passage from the music itself and decorate that to highlight particular words or phrases. Alternatively, several pieces of music, and perhaps all the works of your favourite composer, could be placed in the same frame, and there are many variations on this theme that you can follow. You may even be able to use flowers that are native to the particular country in which the composer in question was born, or match the flowers to the piece of music – you could choose a selection of country flowers for a pastoral composition, for example.

In this photograph I decorated the *Abide With Me* sheet with thalictrum leaves, as their shape is so pretty, and added some frothy alchemilla flowers. The large flowers are the shrub rose 'Canary Bird'. I used a very interesting rectangular frame, with a marquetry inlay. The rich orange colour of the wood tones beautifully with the yellow roses and gives a distinctive period feel to the finished picture.

The frontispiece from a copy of the music from the Peer Gynt suite by Grieg was a beautiful piece of artwork even before it was decorated, so I only arranged some flowers in two of the corners, rather than all

the way round, which would have overpowered the original design. I used some leaves and tendrils from old man's beard, some rose leaves, alchemilla flowers, dark pink Japanese anemones, 'Ballerina' roses and some *Alchemilla alpina* leaves. This piece needed a simpler frame, and so I chose a fairly straightforward gold frame that would harmonise with, rather than detract from, the overall design.

You can use this idea to decorate other printed items that have a sentimental meaning, such as theatre programmes, menus and invitations. You could even press the flowers that were worn or used at the event and then use them as the decoration.

For example, to commemorate a wedding, you could press some of the flowers carried by the bride in her bouquet, and then use them to decorate a sheet of the music played at the wedding. Alternatively, you could decorate the order of service, if one was printed, or even write out the words of one of the hymns used and frame it with a selection of the pressed flowers.

Other important pieces of music can be remembered in the same way. If you know someone who has just passed a very difficult music exam, for instance, you could celebrate their victory by decorating some of their exam piece with a few pressed flowers before framing it and giving it.

Of course, if you are musical yourself, then what a wonderful excuse it would be for composing a tune for someone special and writing it out neatly on manuscript paper. You could use both an ink and a paper that tones in with the pressed flowers, such as some lovely parchment and a sepia-coloured ink, with some pressed flowers in shades that are rich but evocative of days gone by.

Decorating a sheet of music with some pressed flowers is a charming and most unusual way of remembering a favourite song or composer.

PHOTOGRAPH MOUNTS

Pictures of one's family are a treasured item in any home, and this is an idea for turning a small but favourite picture into a more decorative item.

There are two ways in which you can achieve this look. First, as shown in the photograph on the facing page, the flowers can be glued on to the mount board and then protected with a glass frame, or they can be covered with a sheet of cold-seal film before framing. Although the latter method makes the mount far less delicate whenever it is handled, I feel that the cold-seal film detracts from the beauty of the flowers and that simple glueing is far superior – you will just have to take a little more care when handling the finished product.

Having chosen the photograph that you wish to display, you must then decide on the amount of card with which you wish to surround it. In this case I chose a mount measuring approximately 17.5cm (7in) square, with a 7.5-cm (3-in) diameter aperture. Be careful to choose a pale-coloured piece of card if you will be using dark flowers, and if you wish to use some white or light-coloured flowers, you should choose a card in a dark colour such as brown, black or navy. Generally speaking, one is best avoiding the middle colour tones as they will not blend well with the flowers.

Having laid out the design, you should then apply the rubber adhesive solution (egg white is probably not strong enough for this job). You must do this very thoroughly, as the picture will not be as tightly secured against the glass if it only has a free-standing photograph frame backing as opposed to the hardboard backing one uses for normal pictures. Once the glue is dry you should place the photograph in the correct position, securing it with masking tape. Then scrupulously clean the glass as usual, and assemble all the components together in the frame.

One of the benefits of decorated photograph frames is that one can always alter the surround at will, thereby changing the colour emphasis of a particular photograph. You could even make a different arrangement for each season, if you are decorating a photograph you wish to keep displayed all year round.

You can also use this idea for other photographs that you might not otherwise have put out on display. If you are lucky enough to own any old sepia family photographs, it can look extremely attractive to arrange a collection of them on a wall, as you can then give them all co-ordinating mounts that are decorated with your favourite pressed flowers, or perhaps choose some flowers that are appropriate to the family.

Wedding photographs also look lovely when given a floral border, and particularly if you can press some of the flowers from the wedding bouquet. If you wish to use the wedding flowers but they have long since passed their best, you could choose a suitable selection from a florist or your garden and press those. Alternatively, you could press some similar flowers in the same colourings and use those to decorate the picture. Small babies always look lovely in photographs, regardless of the surround, but you could make the picture of a new baby even more special by decorating it with a pretty mount.

If you are sending photographs abroad for some friends or relatives, then why not send some local flowers, or some from your garden, as a reminder not only of your family but also of your home or country. If you have already pressed and arranged the flowers on a mount, the recipient will be able to assemble their own picture rather than take the risk of a glass frame smashing during its journey through the post and damaging the picture.

The card background I used for this photo frame was an extremely pale peachy pink, on which I placed some rose leaves, heuchera flowers and green spiky leaves, with 'Marjorie Fair' and 'Yesterday' roses forming the central focus.

Making a Traditional Sampler

I had the idea for this design one day when I was working on some embroidery. It takes a great deal of time to embroider a sampler in silks or wools, but it is a much swifter process when using pressed flowers. There is also the bonus of pressed flowers being a very unusual medium with which to work.

Of course there is a wide variety of sayings that one could choose, as well as such traditional styles as alphabets, or one's name and the date on which the sampler was completed. I chose 'Home Sweet Home' as it is a relatively short saying and very traditional. For the background of this design I found a rough raw silk which I felt looked much better than the more conventional old linen, but one could always choose one of the linen-covered mountboards that are available in similar colourings, or even hessian or plain linen.

The fabric is cut to the size of the glass, although you must be careful to ensure that the grain of the fabric runs in a straight line, otherwise it is very obvious and will distract from the finished design. In this case, the rectangular frame was used in a sideways, or landscape, position, rather than upright, or portrait, as it balanced the wording better. However, if one was creating a sampler bearing, say, rows of the letters of the alphabet, then one would use the frame the other way round.

Position the wording first, as the outer designs can be altered to suit the space available. For this sampler, I used the centres from potentillas to form the letters, but there are many alternatives. For example, the small flowers borne by laurel bushes look like little black crosses, and therefore remarkably like cross-stitch. You could also use such tiny flower heads as forget-me-nots, or even small, whole, potentillas. However, you must remember to choose plant material that is sufficiently small to give a clear outline, otherwise what you hoped would be an easily read message will look more like an illegible jumble.

Having laid out the wording, you should then appraise the space left around it and choose a suitable design. Here, I used four different designs as they add interest, but they could easily have been four matching designs. In the top left-hand corner I used thalictrum leaves with some alchemilla flowers, and chose potentilla 'Miss Willmott' for the main flowers. The top right-hand corner was decorated with small rose leaves interspersed with some ladies' bedstraw, on which I arranged some geums and cow parsley centres. For the bottom right-hand corner I chose some rose leaves with alchemilla and Japanese anemones, and the bottom left-hand design used some agrimony leaves with astrantia and single red roses. Finally, I chose a new frame for its lovely country feel.

Don't worry if at first you are hard-pressed for inspiration, as looking through old books of sampler designs, needlework and embroidery books should provide you with a wealth of ideas. It's astonishing how the two crafts can mix together, and I constantly find that needlework and pressed flower work complement each other.

As with so many of the ideas shown in this book, a sampler made from pressed flowers would make a stunning gift. If a newly married couple are moving into their first home, for example, you could create a design incorporating both their names, the date of their move and perhaps even the name or location of their house. A sampler commemorating the birth of a new baby also makes a marvellous present for the proud parents, or even grandparents. Once you begin working, you will find that the possibilities are endless.

You can elaborate on this sampler idea by putting the words inside another design. For instance, you could arrange a garland or archway of flowers around the words, or even just a rectangular border and still create the designs in each corner. If using a longer message or saying, you could insert thin decorative lines between each line of text.

THE FOUR SEASONS

Once you begin working with pressed flowers, you may find that you have the same problem that I still face every time I start a new design – I always want to use as much of my pressed material as possible, if not the whole lot! If that is the case, you will find that reproducing this Four Seasons design will at least give you the chance to use four different colour themes and to create four little pictures within one frame.

There is no need to be too rigid in your choice of material for each season, unless you feel it is important, but nevertheless you should still maintain the overall feeling of each season, although in some cases I chose a few out-of-season flowers to give a better colour or shape. If you do want to only mix flowers by correct season, you will have to take care when combining large and little flowers, such as daffodils and snowdrops, as the size difference seems even more pronounced once the flowers have been pressed flat. Another point to remember is that if all four pictures are to sit comfortably together in the overall design, then all the material used should be of roughly the same size. It will look very strange if you choose a single, and extremely large, flower with a few wispy pieces of foliage for one season, while the next is a furious mix of masses of tiny alpine flowers and foliage.

Having decided to show all the four seasons in one picture (as opposed to other occasions when I have made them as a matching set of four separate pictures), I had to find a mount that would blend well with all the seasons and colours, so chose an earthy brown. I used a shade that is lighter than most soils, although of course I am used to looking out of the window at our bright reddish-brown soil here in Devon! I then drew some gold lines between the square apertures to give some definition and help separate the four designs.

The frame also had to harmonise with the mount, as well as draw the eye outwards to give the picture a feeling of solidity. Had I chosen anything smaller or narrower, the picture would have looked slightly fussy or muddled. The brown and gold moulding also made the frame an ideal choice, as it harmonised with both the mount and the gold lines.

When creating the flower pictures themselves, I made the spring and summer designs, on the top row, curve towards each other to form a complementary pair, and used the same effect for the bottom row of autumn and winter. This helps to balance the overall picture, rather than create four completely random designs.

For the spring picture (top left-hand corner), I used some small wild clematis leaves, tendrils of old man's beard, snowdrops, sprays of forget-me-not flowers, red and white hawthorn flowers and some *Alchemilla alpina* leaves.

When working on the summer picture (top right-hand corner), I chose some very small wild rose leaves, some pieces of Russian vine and sea lavender with sprays of alchemilla flowers. The flowers in the centre of the design are small wild or dog roses, yellow potentillas and some pink larkspur.

The autumn design is composed of some brown fern-like leaves that came from a tree at the bottom of my garden, some tiny pieces of Japanese maple, some elderflower buds, gorse flowers, a few tagetes, some hydrangea florets and some 'Red Ace' potentillas.

Unless you are lucky enough to live somewhere that's warm in the winter, you could find it difficult to choose a good selection of flowers for this particular design. Here, I have certainly cheated to obtain the effect I wanted, using ivy and conifer leaves with some pink heather, some pink-edged creamy spray carnations and some bright red verbena.

Creating a design of this type affords you plenty of scope in choosing pressed flowers and colour schemes, but you must ensure that they complement the mount and frame.

A Pressed Flower Mirror

Mirrors can be very attractive wall decorations in their own right, although there are others that seem to be lacking a certain something. If so, then decorating a sheet of mirrored glass with a few pressed flowers and framing the result can transform a useful household item into a unique and extremely attractive decorative feature. You can work with any size of mirror, from minute to enormous, and it can be free-standing to sit on top of a dressing table or hung on a wall, as shown in the photograph on the opposite page.

First choose the size of mirror that you want and then have a sheet of mirrored glass cut to your specifications. Then, create the design actually on the glass itself, before fixing it in place very firmly and thoroughly with rubber adhesive solution.

Assuming that you have managed to secure the pieces without any glue showing, the trickiest part of the operation comes next: you must now ensure that the mirror is scrupulously clean and free from dust. This is a good deal more difficult than it sounds, as small pieces of fluff and hairs always seem to appear from thin air by the million and float down on to the glass! Make sure you use a cloth that is free from any lint, and take great care when cleaning off any fingerprints from the mirror that you do not damage the pressed flower design. Having cleaned the mirror surface as well as you can, you must then cover it with a sheet of clear glass cut to the same size, that has also been well cleaned.

Once you have covered the mirror with the glass you may well find that several pieces of fluff have been trapped between the two, and are being magnified by both the mirror and the covering glass. In this case, your only option is to lift up the glass, remove the offending items and try again. It is nigh on impossible to get the mirror and glass completely clean, so you will have to make a slight compromise by accepting that there will always be a certain amount of dust caught between the two layers of glass, due to static electricity.

For this mirror, I chose a design consisting of a bed of silverweed leaves, interspersed with some ferns and grasses. I then used some lovely red single shrub roses and some white Japanese anemones, placed upside down to take advantage of their silky backs, with some potentilla centres.

You will see that I placed the two arrangements diagonally opposite from each other, but of course you can alter this to a continuous design around the edge, leaving the centre of the mirror free, or simply decorate the bottom of the mirror, leaving the rest free for its original purpose!

This is a marvellous opportunity for making a mirror that exactly blends in with the design and colour scheme of a particular room. For instance, it would make a most attractive addition to a feminine bedroom, or add a much-needed softening touch to a rather austere bathroom or cloakroom.

When making a pressed flower mirror you must ensure that you choose a fairly sturdy frame, with a reasonable depth of rebate. This is because the frame will have to accommodate not only the thickness of the plain glass but also the thickness of the mirror and that of the hardboard backing. You must also bear in mind that the combination of the mirror and glass will make the finished article twice as heavy as it would normally be, and therefore the frame must be able to take this excess weight.

Finally, when you are hanging the mirror, do remember to use some extra-sturdy hooks and nylon picture cord, as it will be heavier than a normal mirror, and you don't want to ruin your carefully constructed design, as well as incur seven years' bad luck, by watching the whole thing smash on to the floor!

Making a mirror that is decorated with pressed flowers is an ideal way of co-ordinating the decorative scheme of a room, and it would also be a perfect gift.

ACKNOWLEDGEMENTS

The Publishers would like to thank the following for their help and advice:

Edward Bunting and family

Chinacraft of London, 499 Oxford Street, London W1 and branches for the loan of china

Jane Churchill, 135 Sloane Street, London SW1X 9AY, for supplying fabrics and wallpapers

The Cloth Shop, 49 Brewer Street, London W1, for supplying fabrics

Colefax and Fowler, 307 Merton Road, London SW18 5JS, for supplying fabrics and wallpapers

Coloroll Limited, Wallcoverings Division, Riverside Mills, Crawford Street, Nelson, Lancs BB9 7QT, for supplying wallpapers

The Covent Garden General Stores, 107–115 Long Acre, Covent Garden, London WC2, for the loan of china

S Double A Mouldings, 12 Boscawen Road, Falmouth, Cornwall, for providing frames

Falkiner Fine Art Paper Limited, 76 Southampton Row, London WC1, for supplying papers

Hamilworth Floral Products Limited, 23 Lime Road, Dumbarton, Dunbartonshire G82 2RP, for supplying ribbons

L A Accessories, 87–95 Cleveland Street, London W1P 6JL, for supplying ribbons, tags, tassels and cords

Luxury Needlepoint, Beauchamp Place, London W1, for supplying tapestry materials

My Fair Lady of Covent Garden, for supplying fresh flowers

Moyses Stevens, 6 Bruton Street, London W1X 7AG, for supplying fresh flowers

Next Limited, 9 South Moulton Street, London W1, for supplying wallpapers

Offray Ribbon Limited, Ashbury, Roscrea, County Tipperary, Ireland, for supplying ribbons

Penny Farthing Gallery, Torquay, Devon, for cutting the mounts

Julie Prowse Fabrics Limited, 1st floor, 4 Farm Street, London W1X 7RA, for supplying fabrics

Pronuptia, 70–78 York Way, London N1 9AG, for the loan of wedding gloves and parasol

Lady Salisbury for permission to reproduce the photograph of Hatfield House by Hugh Palmer

Sanderson, 52–53 Berners Street, London W1P 3AD, for supplying wallpapers and fabrics

Scallywag, 187–191 Clapham Road, Stockwell, London SW9, for supplying pine furniture

Margaret Thorpe for supplying the fresh flower bouquets

John Waggett, QuadruGraphics Limited, Soho Mill, Wooburn Green, High Wycombe, Bucks HP10 0PP, for framing consultation, text and materials

Warner & Sons Limited, Waverley House, 7–11 Noel Street, London W1 4AL, for supplying fabrics

Wren Loasby Designs, Brennels Mead, Highweek, Newton Abbot, for cutting the stencils

Robert Young Antiques, 68 Battersea Bridge Road, London SW11, for the loan of antiques

The publishers would like to thank the following for their permission to use their photographs

Hugh Palmer: p. 21; p. 23 top; p. 25
Photos Horticultural Picture Library: p. 23 bottom; p. 24; p. 26; p. 27; p. 28
Zefa Photo Library (UK) Limited: p. 31

For further details and a catalogue of Joanna Sheen's pressed flower pictures, write to:

Joanna Sheen Limited
PO Box 52
Newton Abbot
Devon